Women Among Monuments

Women Among Monuments

Solitude, Permission, and the Pursuit of Female Genius

KASIA VAN SCHAIK

DUNDURN PRESS

Publisher and acquiring editor: Meghan Macdonald
Cover designer: Laura Boyle
Cover image: Portrait photograph of Georgia O'Keeffe by Alfred Stieglitz, 1918

Library and Archives Canada Cataloguing in Publication

Title: Women among monuments : solitude, permission, and the pursuit of female genius / Kasia Van Schaik.
Names: Van Schaik, Kasia, author.
Description: Includes bibliographical references and index.
Identifiers: Canadiana (print) 20250281198 | Canadiana (ebook) 20250281201 | ISBN 9781459752627 (softcover) | ISBN 9781459752634 (PDF) | ISBN 9781459752641 (EPUB)
Subjects: LCSH: Creative ability in women. | LCSH: Gifted women—Psychology. | LCSH: Women artists—Biography. | LCSH: Women authors—Biography. | LCSH: Artists—Biography. | LCSH: Authors—Biography.
Classification: LCC BF416.A1 V36 2026 | DDC 153.3/5082—dc23

We acknowledge the support of the Canada Council for the Arts and the Ontario Arts Council for our publishing program. We also acknowledge the financial support of the Government of Ontario, through the Ontario Book Publishing Tax Credit and Ontario Creates, and the Government of Canada.

Printed and bound in Canada.

Dundurn Press
1382 Queen Street East
Toronto, Ontario, Canada M4L 1C9
dundurn.com, @dundurnpress

The important thing is that we have raised the debate about the under-representation of women among monuments and it is now very clear to all politicians that we need a very good statue of a woman in a very good place.

— MARGHERITA COLONNELLO, city councillor,
Padua, Italy, interviewed by *The Guardian*, 2022

Contents

Preface

First Woman Ph.D.

THIS STORY BEGINS IN 2022, PADUA, MIDWINTER. ACROSS the city a debate is raging. It concerns a woman whose name I only recently learned: Elena Lucrezia Cornaro Piscopia, the first woman in the world to earn a Ph.D. City councillors Margherita Colonnello and Simone Pillitteri have proposed to place a statue of Piscopia in the town square — a notable historical woman to join the effigies of notable historical men. This suggestion has sparked outrage across the country.

It hadn't occurred to me to type "first woman Ph.D." into Google. I kicked myself for my lack of curiosity. After all, I was going to be the first woman in my family to earn a doctorate. It had been the hardest thing I'd attempted in my life so far, partly because I still felt, deep down, that I wasn't entitled to the pursuit of an intellectual or creative life. I felt I was getting away with something, fooling the academy, and it was only a matter of time until I was exposed. As I've come to understand, this isn't an uncommon experience, particularly for first-generation scholars, or scholars who have disabilities, or who identify as queer, BIPOC, or women.

I wondered if Piscopia had felt this way, too. As a woman in the 1600s, she'd had to fight for her education. Piscopia was born to unmarried parents, a peasant woman and a nobleman. Her father tried to arrange betrothals for his daughter, but she rebuffed each suitor's advances, preferring the company of her harpsicord and philosophy books. Women weren't allowed to enter university at the time, but her father was able to pull a few strings for his prodigious daughter. Even then, the residing Cardinal Gregorio Barbarigo opposed Piscopia's request to graduate with a doctorate in theology, arguing that it was a "mistake" for a woman to become a "doctor." He eventually let her graduate with a degree in philosophy instead. Also, because she was a woman, she wasn't permitted to lecture at the university. Italy was still governed by Paul the Apostle's dictum that a woman wasn't allowed to "teach, nor to usurp authority over the man, but to be in silence."[1]

I looked up the year 1678. *Le Griffon*, the first European ship to sail on the Great Lakes of North America, prepares for her maiden voyage. The first fire engine company in what will become the United States goes into service in Boston. *The Pilgrim's Progress*, a text that 334 years later I'd be forced to read in an undergraduate literature class, is published in London, England. Rebel Chinese general Wu Sangui takes the imperial crown and dies of dysentery months later; Franco-Dutch battles are instigated, ceasefires called, and in Padua, at the age of thirty-two, Piscopia receives her Ph.D.

• • •

At almost 90,000 square metres, Prato della Valle, or "Meadow of the Valley," is the second-largest square in Europe. At its centre is a green island surrounded by a small canal and bordered by two rings of statues, all of historical men. I recognize some of the names: Galileo, father of observable astronomy; the artist Mantegna, famous for his use of perspective and anatomical detail; the long-suffering sonneteer Petrarch, granddad of unrequited love poems; and the eighteenth-century sculptor Canova, renowned for turning stone into flesh.[2]

Two of the pedestals in Padua's elliptical square are empty, their statues destroyed by Napoleon's army after it conquered the Republic of Venice. It seemed fitting, the city councillors proposed, that Piscopia might rest on one of the empty pedestals, that hers might become the first monument honouring a woman in the city's historic centre. As art historian Federica Arcoraci points out, spending time among the square's all-male statues has "an impact on our lives and collective imagination," and the "Prato della Valle regulation of 1776 never … prohibited the representation of women."[3]

Across the country, critics protested Piscopia's inclusion in the square. Some claimed that a statue of the first woman Ph.D. would be out of context with the square's history. They argued that the pedestals, the ones that once belonged to the destroyed statues, should remain empty, since they were symbols of Italy's perseverance against Napoleon's troops. Others believed that to include a female statue within the pantheon of male statues would be an act of "cancel culture."

In an interview with *The New York Times*, Colonnello confessed that the enormous backlash to their proposal had come as a surprise. The national outrage reflected the reality that, while things were changing in Italy, there remained those who didn't understand the importance of discussing the underrepresentation of half the country's population. Colonnello and Pillitteri walked back their original proposal, but they still insisted that a statue of a woman be allowed in the square. It didn't have to be Piscopia — they were willing to erect her monument elsewhere. But the city had to decide on another historical woman instead — for instance, the nineteenth-century painter Elisabetta Benato-Beltrami or the writer Gualberta Alaide Beccari.

"The important thing," said Colonnello, "is that we have raised the debate about the underrepresentation of women among monuments and it is now very clear to all politicians that we need a very good statue of a woman in a very good place." She pressed on: "We now need to decide where and who. But I think we will eventually settle on the square — it is very huge and there is lots of space."[4]

I looked up an image of Prato della Valle. Colonnello is right. At the size of almost two football fields, it's massive.

Why was there such opposition to the inclusion of a woman in such an enormous space? It appeared that the controversy wasn't about the square itself but what the square symbolized. It represented the boys' club, cultural memory, the legacy of genius. The square represented representation itself.

What the Piscopia debate exposed wasn't just the scarcity of statues celebrating notable women — of the thousands of statues in Italy, fewer than two hundred depict women — but the historical resistance to simply recognizing women's achievements. This resistance isn't unique to Italy.

After reading about Elena Piscopia, I went walking through the squares, parks, and boulevards of Montreal, my own city. This was where I'd lived for much of my life — a place I kept returning to for its promise of art, freedom, and community. Yet, like the Prato della Valle, it was still filled with statues of European men.

Where were the women? I found myself asking this as I stood below the Sir George-Étienne Cartier monument at the foot of Mont Royal. Not the angels and goddesses but the monuments to historical women. Where could I find them?

• • •

It was around this time that I received a call from an old friend from my master's program, whom I hadn't seen in over ten years. She'd be in Montreal for a visit and had some books she wished to return to me.

The last time we'd seen each other was right before I left Canada for Europe. I was in my mid-twenties then and living with seven roommates in a Toronto townhouse. I'd received a small writing grant and had booked a one-way ticket to Berlin. I didn't know when or if I'd return. I hosted a party in my backyard and invited everyone I knew. On the grass lay all my worldly possessions, including my steel-string guitar, most of my clothes, and all my books. I asked my friends and acquaintances to take what they wanted. The books were the hardest to part with. I wrote my initials in them before giving them away in the hope that some of them would find me again, but I didn't expect that they would.

My friend and I met in a plant-filled café in Montreal's Quartier des Spectacles. After our initial hugs and hellos, she thrust a package into my hands. "Here," she said, "remember these?"

The package contained several of my old theory textbooks from my undergrad gender studies course, including a dog-eared copy of Virginia Woolf's *A Room of One's Own*. Paging through the slim volume, I recognized with sudden familiarity my own handwriting in the margins. Although I'd read and owned other copies of this book over the years, there was something singular about the first copy. It was as if the pages contained traces of that initial revelatory reading experience.

Later that night, as I reread my long-lost book, it occurred to me that Woolf was asking the same questions I was, except she was asking them a hundred years ago: *Where are the women among monuments? Why aren't there more of them?*

For Woolf, the answer was rooted in the conditions required for pursuing an intellectual and creative life: Women need money and a room of their own to make art. Meet those conditions and the monuments will follow.

But I noticed another element of her argument this time. Woolf's manifesto concludes with a vision for the future woman writer: that in addition to acquiring "five hundred a year each of us and rooms of our own," women should each strive to secure "the habit of freedom" for their creative practice.[5]

It is this second instruction, the "habit of freedom," that caught my attention. What did she mean by this?

Although space and money are deciding factors in creating art, there is also, for women especially, the question of self-worth — the question of permission — to even claim the room and the time spent in it. This, I believed, is what Woolf meant by freedom. Freedom from continual, harmful self-doubt and self-censorship. Freedom to drop out of time. Elena Piscopia alone with her books.

The following chapters examine the long-standing refusal to recognize women among monuments by looking at women writers' and artists' past and present relationships to solitude, self-permission, and ambition. They attempt to imagine environments and alternative domestic structures — the artist's retreat, the unbuilt feminist city — that might offer historically marginalized individuals a chance at a creative life.

Such imaginings prompt new and ongoing questions. What is a creative life? What does such a life look like for women? Where does the inner flint of artistic permission come from? How is it ignited, and what is the oxygen that keeps it burning?

• • •

This book doesn't attempt to be definitive or comprehensive in answering these questions. It's meant to be exploratory, opening doors into new rooms, opening windows onto new vistas to allow for wilder flights of thought. At its heart, this book is a record of chance encounters in late-night kitchens or galleries or in the pages of borrowed books, with writers and artists who have left an impression on my thinking. The surrealist painter Leonora Carrington once observed that for the writer "the task of the right eye is to peer into the telescope, while the left eye peers into the microscope."[6] Thus, one eye pressed to the telescope, the other to the microscope, I trace my own journey alongside those of these writers and artists in an attempt to understand what it means to sustain a creative life.[7]

Although the book focuses primarily on twentieth-century, cisgendered women writers and artists, the titular women in "women among monuments" describes all individuals who identify as women.[8] It is possible that some of the artists in this book may have identified differently had they lived in the twenty-first century. It is possible that in future epochs we might do away with the term *woman* altogether, considering it to be too limiting a category. I thus write this book knowing that language is imperfect and evolving, and that this is what compels me to keep writing: the knowledge that imperfection is a sign of movement, of life.

• • •

And what of the square in Padua? Its story is ongoing as well. By the end of February 2022, after a prolonged debate, Padua's city council approved the motion to place a statue of Elena Piscopia, the first woman Ph.D., on a plinth in Prato della Valle. But as I write this three years later, Piscopia still remains absent from the ring of statues. Visitors can find her statue at the university, preserved behind glass. Perhaps by the time this book is published, her monument will finally be erected in the square.

1

Arrival

ON OUR FIRST MORNING IN CANADA, MY YOUNGER BROTHER and sister and I woke up early. We put on our shoes, and while my mother was still sleeping, left the narrow Victorian townhouse we'd arrived at the night before. Not that we had any memory of that evening, landing at an airport in Spokane, Washington, and crossing the Canadian border at 2:00 a.m. in the back seat of a station wagon only half awake. Outside the front door of the Victorian townhouse lay an unfamiliar mountain community made up of paved streets and tall trees. All the streets sloped down the hillside toward a large shining lake whose glacier-fed waters, we'd learn later, were as cold as the Atlantic Ocean off Cape Town's west-facing beaches. But the water here was different from any water we'd seen, lying flat and dark as lacquered hair, glistening in the cold light of the northern hemisphere. And the streets were different, too — so clean and empty, each lined with blazing red and yellow trees. We were unfamiliar with this season and the name given to it: fall. Because everything is falling, I explained to my siblings, who were a few years younger than me and accepted everything I told them as fact. We were used to thorn trees and aloes, apricot orchards that flowered on my birthday in spring, but all that had changed. The seasons had unfixed themselves from our birthdays, from Christmas and Easter; I was now born in the dying season.

The streets led us past houses made of wood, painted all kinds of colours — blue, maroon, yellow, not the white plaster-washed clay and stone structures we were accustomed to in our village. Cats observed us from windowsills, as if through surveillance screens. A car climbed up the street, the children in the back seat staring at us without waving. We continued up the pavement — in this new world it was called a sidewalk — looking in on the empty yards and front porches, their identical wind chimes and drawn curtains reflecting our foreignness back at us. After about an hour of walking through the small mountain town — though at the time it seemed enormous compared to the village we'd just moved from — my brother stopped and sat on the curb.

"I'm hungry," he announced. "Can we go home now?"

My sister said nothing, but she stopped, too, and gazed up and down the street. "Where are we?" she asked at last.

Up ahead, a man in a fleece vest peeled out of a driveway with two small boys, one in a carrier, the other with a soccer ball under his arm. As we approached them, the man frowned at us over wire-framed glasses. I don't recall what we asked him, but I remember he didn't understand us at first. Our accents were too thick. We repeated ourselves, explaining that we were lost.

"Where do you live?" the man asked. "Do you remember your address?"

I realized then that I didn't know our house number or the name of our street, but I did recollect that the woman who had picked us up from the airport the night before had told our mother we'd be living on the steepest street in the town. I told the man this now. "Which is the steepest street?"

"They're all pretty steep," the man said, peering up the hill. "Maybe Josephine? Or Hendryx? Or Cedar? But they're long streets."

He pointed up to where the streets began, high on the hill, and down to where they ended, nearly at the water's edge.

"But which is the steepest?" I asked, as if the street gradient of the town should be common knowledge among its inhabitants.

The man shrugged helplessly. He said he couldn't tell us objectively what was the steepest but offered to walk us to Cedar, which was in the direction he was going. Once we found Cedar Street, we thanked the man and his kids, and starting at the top, walked down its precipitous sidewalk, carefully studying each narrow Victorian house, searching for a red mailbox, a broken front step, which were the only identifying details we could recall about the house. After about thirty minutes, my sister pointed out a house with a red door, and though we still weren't convinced it was the right one, we tried it. The door was unlocked. There, in the hall, stood four unpacked suitcases. But even then we weren't sure we'd entered the right house. Perhaps those suitcases belonged to another set of children who had also just arrived from the other side of the world and we were trespassing in their house. We continued to feel unsure until we found, in a dark room at the top of the stairs, our mother still asleep.

• • •

Although this took place more than half a lifetime ago, I still remember that prickly awareness starting at the back of my neck and moving to my face and arms, the growing realization that we were utterly and irrevocably lost. My siblings had followed me blindly. I'd neglected to plant the breadcrumbs or unspool the red thread. There would be no reversal, no going back to where we came from. Perhaps this is something all travellers, all immigrants, come to realize at some point in their journeys. You can retrace your steps back among the monuments of your past, through empty public squares and silent architecture, but you can never really return.

Since that first great dislocation, I've moved frequently. I've left cities I've lived in and returned to find their shapes and moods altered — sometimes so significantly that they're almost unrecognizable to me — but I've seldom felt so deeply that sensation of being lost as I did that first day in Canada. And in the years following, of being alone.

In South Africa, we'd been surrounded by community, friends, neighbours, and queer family. Here we were strangers.

During our first year in Canada, we moved into a rental on the outskirts of the city. My mother worked long hours, often returning home late in the evening. I remember mice in the walls at night; the quiet, mostly unfurnished rooms; the flat, unblinking eye of a neighbour's trampoline; eventually a seasonal affective disorder diagnosis. But most of all I recall the hours alone.

It was this aloneness that led me to making art. First drawing and painting, then writing songs, and finally writing poetry and fiction. It was as if a vacuum had opened up in our lives and the only way to avoid being sucked over its event horizon was by inventing something new every day, a story, a song, a drawing. This was the bargain.

It was around this time that I started listening to Joni Mitchell, who, I learned, had also grown up in Canada. What captivated me most was her storytelling — her ability to express a world, a scene, the coordinates of a whole life, in a few lines of verse. There was one song in particular, "A Case of You," that I listened to on repeat. The third verse opens with a line about being a lonely painter and living inside a box of paints.

It was this image of the painter who lived in her art, and for her art, that enchanted me. The artist who could both fill up the room with her voice and shrink to the size of a paintbrush, who could be both vulnerable and brave.

Was art a defence against loneliness? I wondered as I strummed my guitar along to Mitchell's voice. Or was it a product of loneliness? Was it both?

• • •

Recently, on a phone call with my mother, we talked about our first year in Canada. It had been one of the most stressful years of her life. The demands of the new teaching job, the culture shock, the sudden absence of friends and family, had come as an assault to her system, and our family. I asked her if she regretted the move. Back then, she said, she had no time to think of regret. But, she added, when she finally returned to South Africa decades later to see her mother, she'd wondered if she'd made a mistake to give up community, family, friends, and year-round sunshine for the economic opportunity and safety Canada promised. And the winter, she declared, those months and months of winter. She paused for a moment and then said: "I asked myself, have I wasted my life? But you can't think of it like that, can you? It's the life we lived, that we are still living, so it cannot be a wasted life."

2

Next Picasso

1

SHORTLY AFTER OUR ARRIVAL IN CANADA, I WAS VOTED "Next Picasso" in my high school yearbook. This was due to my ability to draw hands. As any student of art knows, hands are notoriously difficult, but I'd spent a lot of time looking at mine, clasped tightly in my lap, while larger decisions were made over my head like: *Should we move across the world to make a better life?* I'd also spent a lot of time examining God's hands in Michelangelo's *The Creation of Adam*, which was laminated and pasted across the back wall of my high school art class. I'd stare at it during lunch hours spent alone in the art room and think about how lucky God was that he got to bring his entourage along with him inside his big red cape. I'd had to leave all my friends behind in a rural town in the Western Cape.

Other than God and Adam's lazy reach for the touch that would spark life, two things struck me about this painting: Adam's small triangular penis and the presence of a naked woman under God's arm. Who was she? Eve, awaiting her own

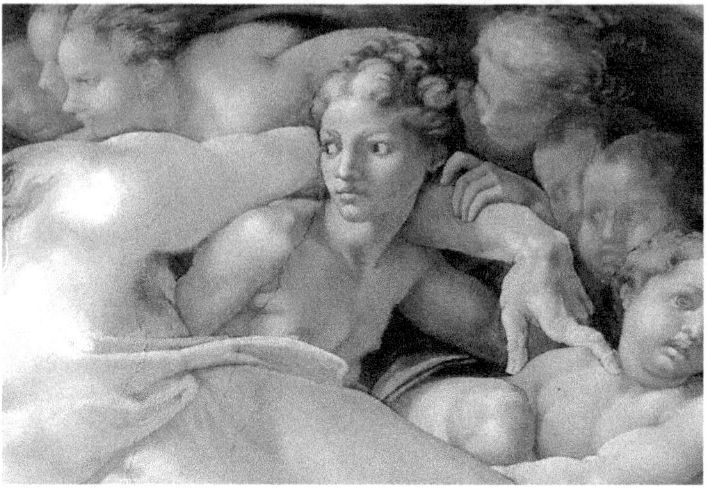

The figure under God's arm.

chance at existence? The unnamed woman eyes Adam warily, unsure of what her role in history will be and whether there's room for her on his green slab of rock.

Upon closer inspection, I realized the wary figure under God's arm appeared more androgenous. This could be because Michelangelo was notoriously bad at sculpting women. He, like many Renaissance artists, routinely used men as models for depictions of female subjects.[1] Could the watchful face under God's arm belong to a cherub or angel, or even a backup copy of Adam, a Plan B if the first version turned out to be a disappointment? Or perhaps the figure in God's armpit was androgenous because she or they hadn't yet had to go up against a world that would pry their consciousness into a girl-shaped mould.

If the figure was indeed Eve, she was unsocialized, unborn, and not yet blamed for all of humanity's suffering. She wasn't yet made to be a shield or an ornament, to use visual artist and musician Vivek Shraya's phrase.[2] She wasn't yet pinned down by category. I recognized this liquid state. It was how I'd felt as a child in pre-girlhood, moving across the hard and soft surfaces of the world in my corduroys.

After being voted Next Picasso, a popular boy in my math class, coincidentally named Adam, asked if I'd draw his portrait. He met me in the art room during recess and sat across

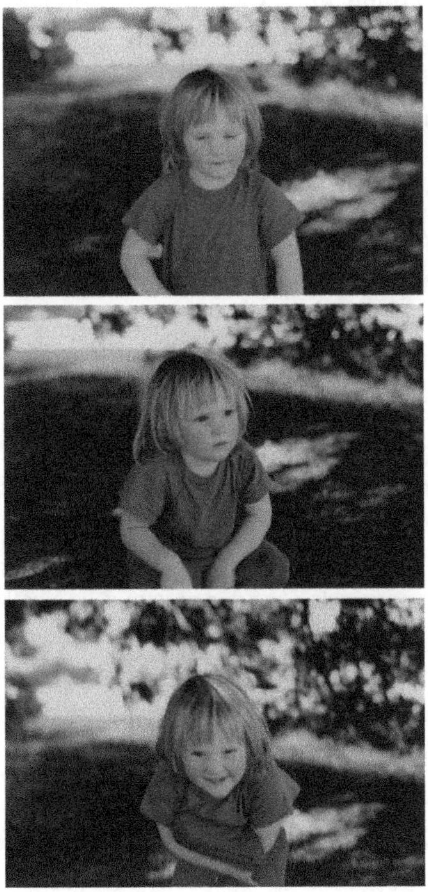

Before girlhood.

the table from me as I sharpened my pencils. We had nothing in common except low grades in algebra, but it was pleasant to be in the presence of this nice-looking, popular boy, to have him fix me with his attention. In soft 2B, I faithfully reproduced his acne scars and frosted tips, which made him look like a sixth member of NSYNC. I was surprised to find that he and the other students knew my name at all. The oldest daughter of a low-income, single-parent immigrant family, I was trying my best to not be noticed, to dilute my accent, and to assimilate, especially after ridiculing myself in front of my entire class on my first day. After making a spelling mistake in my workbook, I'd asked my homeroom table if anyone had a rubber. The room exploded in laughter. *Do you know what that is? A condom!*

Adam gazed around the art room as I sketched his face, his eyes resting on the Michelangelo print on the back wall. I wondered what he thought of his namesake draped across the green rock that was the earth.

"Is that what you want to be when you grow up?" he asked. "An artist?"

I wasn't sure if he was mocking me, so I shrugged and focused on shading in his nostrils. Deep down, I sensed there was something slightly embarrassing or odd about a girl wanting to be an artist. Or maybe it was ambition that I was embarrassed by, the sense of entitlement and self-confidence required to call oneself an artist.

When I completed Adam's portrait, I was dismayed to see that it looked nothing like him. Although I'd carefully reproduced his frosted tips, I hadn't managed to get his facial proportions right. The chin was too rounded, the lips too full. No, it wasn't Adam at all. The face that stared back at me from the page was my own.

• • •

Although I enjoyed the social elevation the yearbook title gave me, I knew there was no way I could be the Next Picasso. First off, I didn't own paints, acrylic or oil. Paris didn't await me. My father wasn't a professor at the Barcelona School of Fine Arts; in fact, there were no plans or money for me to enter university at all. Like Picasso, though, I loved to draw women. I spent my lunch hours in the art room copying out Titian's and Botticelli's obsessive reproductions of Venus.

Knowing how to draw naked women, I believed, was essential to becoming an artist, so I practised every day. I filled five pages of my notebook with breasts. When my peers in my art class noticed my drawings, they taunted me. I ignored them and went on shading in areolas or sketching in the silky black hairs that sometimes sprouted up around them. There was so much variation in the female body. I wanted to be accurate. This, I had decided at sixteen, was the task of an artist.

Sometimes, during lunch break, I'd hook up the projector and trace the image of the tree-lined street that our art teacher, Ms. Hart, had given us to learn perspective. Perspective, she said, pertained to the science of optics that began in the late fourteenth century. The tree-lined image was called *The Avenue at Middelharnis* by Meindert Hobbema, painted in 1689. "There are two kinds of space in painting," read our textbook. "The flat, two-dimensional space of the canvas on which the painter places lines and colours, and the illusion of three-dimensional space, called pictorial space, which is suggested by those shapes, colours, and lines."

I wanted to live in the pictorial space created by Hobbema. I wanted to follow Middelharnis Avenue, which I believed to be in South Africa because the trees looked like eucalyptus, the invasive species in the part of the Karoo where I'd grown up. "As objects get farther away from the viewer they appear to decrease in size at a constant rate," read the textbook. I traced the shrinking avenue. I calculated the decreasing height of each tree to re-create the impression of distance. But I wasn't just learning about illusionary perspective — how to trick the eye into seeing a three-dimensional landscape on a two-dimensional space — I was gaining a fuller understanding of perspective as a point of view. I would use these tools to reproduce drawings by Picasso, Raphael, and Oskar Kokoschka. I still remember painting an interpretation of Kokoschka's trembling blue-and-green portrait, *The Bride of the Wind*. Each work of art, each piece of writing, was created through a point of view, and no point of view was neutral, not for the artwork, not for the artist.

As I sketched out a reproduction of Egon Schiele's *Seated Woman with Legs Drawn Up* for my year-end project, I wondered what effect replicating all these paintings by men had on my brain. How was it shaping the way in which I saw women? I hadn't learned about the male gaze yet, though I had experienced it, both as an object of it, but also inwardly, within my own mechanics of looking. When I coldly searched my body in the mirror for grotesque signs of imperfection, I had the feeling that I'd inherited this gaze. All around me I could sense an ambient desire and disgust for women's bodies.[3] At this point, it was more a feeling of unease, and the study of perspective in art seemed to be compounding this self-interrogation. But even without the vocabulary, I was starting to question where I, or anyone like me, fitted in the history of looking.

2

At the end of the school term, Ms. Hart bought the Egon Schiele reproduction from me for $75. I'd like to say I spent the money on art supplies, but the truth is, I don't remember what I did with it. Once school was out, I'd be working full-time as a nanny and would have no time to draw, anyway.

The family I worked for that summer lived in a 1980s-style McMansion that overlooked the town. There were several entrances to the house — through the marble foyer, or the four-car garage, or the basement, which had a separate suite — and these doors led to hallways, sometimes terminating in vast, empty rooms. On one floor was a marble Jacuzzi tub where I was to bathe my charge, a toddler with a proclivity for gherkins and kalamata olives. On another floor was an enormous playroom filled with handcrafted toys from Germany, and adjacent to that was the kitchen with its unbroken views of the lake. I remember that there was never any good food in their pantry, just rice crackers, chia seeds, and a large supply of pickles. The family kept inviting me to live in their basement suite, to become their twenty-four-hour help, and I had to remind them that I was a high school student and lived with my mom.

It was during the toddler's naps that I first read the Caribbean-American writer Jamaica Kincaid's semi-autobiographical novel *Lucy*.[4] I'd found a copy of it in the public library where I often dropped by on free afternoons. I'd already gone through all the books on the shelf at home, which contained a few early Margaret Atwood novels, a ghost story about an ectopic pregnancy called *The Girl in a Swing*, and a beloved copy of *Wuthering Heights*, given to me by my dad when we still all lived in South Africa (he now lived across the world in New Zealand). I was drawn to *Lucy*'s cover: a bright image of a Tahitian woman painted by the artist Paul Gauguin. In the novel, Lucy Potter, a young girl from Antigua in the West Indies, moves to a New York City suburb to work as an au pair for a wealthy white American family. She's escaping a life walled in by rigid gendered expectations but soon realizes that the United States isn't the land of milk and honey she'd hoped it would be. Lucy finds those rigid gender expectations alive and well in America, especially in the outwardly liberal but privately bigoted household where she works.

When I first read this novel, I felt as if it spoke directly to me. Lucy was also an emigrant and a nanny, and I related to her feelings of alienation and loneliness in North American society. She captured perfectly that uncanny experience of arrival. This understanding goes beyond specific geographies and cities. It's about the arrival in a culture that, though you live in it for decades, doesn't quite fit. Although her experience was very different from my own — Lucy, like her author, had to confront racial biases as well as culture shock — I couldn't shrug that blunt moment of recognition.

• • •

The sense of recognition went beyond emigrant and nanny status. Lucy, too, wanted to be an artist. She, too, felt frustrated. In her spare time, Lucy enrolls in a photography course where she hones her abilities of observation.[5] Wishing to encourage Lucy's artistic inclinations, Lucy's employer, Mariah, brings her to an exhibition of Paul Gauguin's work in the city. But Lucy doesn't see herself in Gauguin's Tahitian women as Mariah anticipated. She recognizes herself in the artist himself. "I identified with the yearnings of this man," she muses.

"I understood finding the place you are born in an unbearable prison and wanting something completely different from what you are familiar with, knowing it represents a haven."

Lucy continues: "I imagined him sitting on a rock smoking a pipe, surrounded by naked women, painting the sunset, but I didn't feel like a naked woman, or even a woman; I felt like a person, like a being, like a consciousness, and I wondered if Gauguin ever felt like that, or if he was always thinking of himself as a man, and his models as women."

This passage stayed with me after I'd finished the book. Like Lucy, I also didn't see myself as the subject of art. I didn't feel like a woman. I felt like a kind of owlish being, a pair of yellow eyes perceiving the world, taking in its rules and customs, swivelling 360 degrees to catch a different point of view. It would surprise me when people addressed me, catcalled, or acknowledged my presence as "woman," breaking the illusion. For a while, I wore the same clothes every day: a pair of loose black pants and a hoodie. I wanted to escape the signifiers that pinpointed me as a muse rather than a thinker or creator. I wanted to watch, not be watched. I wanted to be what Ralph Waldo Emerson called the "Transparent Eyeball," standing barefoot in a top hat and tails on the bare ground, absorbing the world. "I am nothing; I see all." But, of course, I wasn't a transparent eyeball, and I knew I'd never achieve transparent-eyeball status. Neither would Lucy nor any other young woman.[6]

Lucy searches for a model among the monumental artists of the twentieth century but quickly realizes that even female European painters of this time fail her. She becomes fascinated by the paintings of Mary Cassatt, who had studied with the Impressionists in Paris and painted mothers and children and women reading. "Her paintings were like

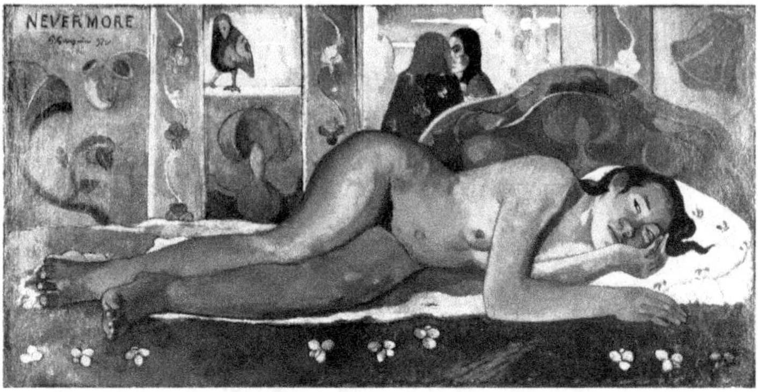

Nevermore (1897) depicts a young woman lying on a bed while a raven watches overhead. She is believed to be Pahura, Paul Gauguin's fifteen-year-old wife, grieving the loss of their first child.

photographs," Lucy notes, "but with a warmth and a tenderness that photographs could never capture. I wanted to be like Mary Cassatt, but I knew I could never be; I was too black, too foreign, too angry."

The novel ends with Lucy in her room alone with a blank notebook in which she inscribes her name: *Lucy Josephine Potter*. She is fuelled by the transformative energy of anger, ready now to pen her own story, to become a writer, an artist.[7] Unlike oil painting, the writer's materials are relatively accessible. As Virginia Woolf once noted, "The cheapness of writing paper is, of course, the reason why women have succeeded as writers before they have succeeded in the other professions."[8]

The image *Lucy* leaves off on is that of a girl in a bedroom with a pen in her hand, writing herself into existence.[9] It was this image that made me feel that I, too, could become a writer, that I could live a creative life.

3

The question of what it takes to live a creative life returned with force some years later when I found myself working as a nanny again. This time it was in Berlin for an American woman who, before the birth of her sons, had been a writer. Was *still* a writer, she corrected herself, during my interview for the job. Each afternoon I took her boys, five-year-old Claude and one-year-old Elio, out into the neighbourhood and bribed them with ice cream and jungle gyms so she could have some hours alone at her desk. Claude was an intelligent, sensitive boy with thick, flaxen hair cut straight across his forehead. He'd been born with a degenerative disease that affected his balance and mobility. Claude had physiotherapy twice a week, which he disliked. He would sometimes fling himself onto the floor in frustration, refusing to move. When he was older, his mother told me, he might require a wheelchair. In preparation for this, his parents had bought an apartment on the ground floor that overlooked a grassy courtyard where Claude could, for the time being, run up and down. This was the time he was happiest, in his own kingdom of the courtyard, and he didn't seem to care that his legs sometimes buckled underneath him.

Beyond the home, it was a different matter. At five, Claude was full of speed, darting into the road ahead of me as I pushed his brother in the stroller up the street. He seemed to challenge the cars to make way for him, to notice his presence in the world, to screech to a stop as he turned back to look at me, racing after him, shouting, "Stop! Claude! Stop!" He had an unusual elasticity to his body, and if we stopped at a playground, he would immediately fling himself onto the monkey bars from which he would fall, his muscles not quick enough to form a grip. I noticed he didn't get along with other children very well, but his younger brother adored him and observed him from the sandbox, pure admiration on his face.

When I came back to the house with the boys, my employer hid in her room, door locked, typing quietly or not typing at all, trying not to give herself away. I'd distract the kids with games and snacks, repeating, "Mummy's not here," though they both knew she was. Somewhere inside their small bodies they felt her presence. Claude, especially. He studied me, frowning, unable to completely immerse himself in play. His worry was contagious. It made me feel as though I, and his mother, had betrayed him. Perhaps this betrayal felt worse because of his condition. On some level, Claude knew he didn't operate within the same time scale as other children. How could we waste this child's precious time with lies? At least this was what I sensed his mother felt, the question she asked herself, the question that deepened her guilt. For her, every moment away from him was a compromise. Was her writing worth that compromise?

In the mornings while Claude was in kindergarten, I'd cart baby Elio to the park in his high-tech stroller. Elio was a very polite baby. Even when on the brink of tears, he'd smile at me apologetically, as if to excuse the brimming emotions he didn't yet understand. Occasionally, he'd nudge himself forward in his stroller and turn his round head of curls to me to point out a bird. "Wawa," he'd say in his deep, serious voice. And I'd agree. "Yes, a wawa."

I noticed that people greeted me when I was with Elio.

"And what is your little boy's name?" they'd ask me. I'd hoist Elio onto my hip so they could see his curls bounce. It was easy to imagine myself as a young mother fulfilling my duty, in the right lane.

"Maybe I should have a baby," I told my roommate when I got home. "Or I could just steal Elio. Do you think that would make me happy? Maybe it's art that makes me sad." By art, I meant creative ambition, the feeling that I wasn't doing enough with my life, or that life was more than just a roster of tasks to complete.[10]

"You just love him because he can't talk," my roommate reminded me. "He's like a pet and can't bore you yet with opinions." She wasn't wrong. On those mornings in the city, Elio was my familiar, companionable and mute. In his company, it was almost like being alone, but I didn't feel lonely.

This was a time when I was constantly composing poems and stories in my head but rarely writing them down. I was too busy chasing children through traffic, but that was only part of it. There was another reason I hadn't committed anything to paper, a reason I didn't want to admit. The unwritten poem, or story or novel, remained ethereal, unmarred by the materiality of the page. There was something sacred about the unwritten poem. It was like the hope I'd seen parents invest in their baby bumps. Each presented a clean slate, nuclei floating astronaut-like in their embryonic sacs, the symbol for a beginning, an origin, a germ of greatness. Perhaps even a germ of genius.

Still, I understood that this kind of thinking was a problem. I couldn't push Elio around in the stroller and compose poems in my head forever. I imagined him expanding in his seat, growing taller in all directions until he finally exited the pram and admonished me in the flawless English he'd learned from listening to me recite my poems, for procrastinating, for using him as an excuse to not write anything down. No, I couldn't continue like this. I needed to find a room where I could participate in the activity called writing, otherwise what was I actually doing? Not-writing. Dreaming.

• • •

But would a room solve all my problems? Physical space was vital, but as Virginia Woolf reminds us, there was also that elusive "habit of freedom." My employer in Berlin had both an office and money enough to hire me to care for her children, but she still seemed to have difficulty believing in her work. She'd resurface from her office after a few hours, face shining with guilt, and hand me my pay as her children stormed her legs. She seemed almost relieved, even thankful, to get back to the task of motherhood. And maybe this wasn't even a task for her. For watching her with her boys I saw a level of love I didn't have in my own life, a fierce, powerful, uncomplicated love that transcended just about everything.

One day my employer told me that before she was married she travelled to Paris alone. Her favourite museum was the Musée de l'Orangerie with Claude Monet's *Water Lilies.* "If you ever go there," she said, "you must visit the Orangerie." It was like the Sistine Chapel. The paintings were larger than life, covering the whole wall, the elliptical rooms creating, in the painter's words, "an illusion of an endless whole, of a wave without horizon and without shore."

My employer recalled feeling elevated by the visit, as if her life had been momentarily opened up. But there was something frightening about being around so much beauty as well, she said. She didn't feel she deserved it.

I understood what she meant. But it wasn't just the feeling of not deserving to be around beauty, or to be an artist, and more the feeling that great art was being made far away in another place, another time. Genius was always elsewhere.

3

Art Monsters in Paris

1

IT WAS ALREADY DARK WHEN I ARRIVED IN PARIS. THE CAB dropped me off at an apartment in the Latin Quarter, and as I rang the doorbell, I hoped my host would allow me to go to sleep immediately.

My arrival at this apartment was more by accident than by design. I hadn't even planned to leave the airport on this stopover — I'd only touched down for a night and would be flying out in the morning — but Élise, a photographer I'd met in Berlin a few weeks earlier, insisted I stay with her cousin.

"Marie-Claude won't mind," said Élise. "I'll call her right now."

Her cousin lived with her boyfriend in one of the coolest neighbourhoods in the city, Élise explained as she waited for Marie-Claude to pick up. Élise herself had stayed with them before; they were very central.

I couldn't follow Élise and Marie-Claude's rapid exchange, but I knew enough basic French vocabulary to determine that my visit posed a problem. Sure enough, it turned out that Marie-Claude was on a trip during the days of my travel and her boyfriend would be alone in the apartment.

"I can just stay at the airport," I said.

Élise shook her head, lapsing into French again. This time I caught a few words.

"No, not pretty at all," she was saying. "Brown hair, average, very average."

Was she describing me?

"You have a place to stay," she announced happily once she hung up. After a pause, she added, "I told my cousin that you are unattractive so that she'd let you stay alone with her boyfriend. You're going to love it," she assured me. "Paris is the most beautiful city in the world. Even Hitler thought so. That's why he didn't destroy it."

My host, the distrusted boyfriend, was a quiet twenty-four-year-old, lanky and bespectacled, with dark, unwashed hair, in his last year of an engineering program. His textbooks lay scattered across the kitchen table. He offered me a glass of water and asked in broken English if I was hungry and seemed relieved when I said I wasn't. The couch was neatly made up with a pillow and a sleeping bag. I was about to head to bed, relieved to get some rest after my transatlantic flight, when the front door flew open. There stood Marie-Claude, home early from her trip, dark eyes flashing around the room, taking inventory. When her gaze landed on me, I wondered if she deemed her cousin's assessment of me accurate — was I ugly enough to be her guest?

"Your first time in Paris!" she exclaimed. "What have you seen so far?"

"Nothing," I told her. "I just arrived and I'll be gone first thing in the morning."

"Oh, no, but you must see Paris," she insisted, and ordered her reluctant boyfriend to bring the car around the front.

It was past midnight when we arrived at the Eiffel Tower. The couple waited in the car as I got out and pointed my camera at the massive structure. I remember falling asleep in the back seat of the car and being prodded awake when we reached the next monument.

I got a few grainy photos of the Arc de Triomphe and the Louvre. As we drove across the city, I glimpsed a glittering river lined with boats, but that could have been a dream because, all of a sudden, I was being nudged awake again by Marie-Claude. We were at the tunnel where Princess Diana died in a car accident the same year my family immigrated to Canada. Erected above the tunnel was a statue of a giant golden flame.

When I got out of the car to take the obligatory picture, I felt something large and soft brush against my leg. A rat shot over the sidewalk and disappeared across the road, heading toward the Seine River. When I returned to the car, Marie-Claude and the engineering student were making out in the front seat, so I waited beside the Flamme de la Liberté until they finished, wondering what the next monument on our midnight tour would be.

As we drove back to the Latin Quarter, Marie-Claude twisted around to look at me. "So what do you think? Isn't it the most beautiful city in the world?"

Although Paris felt shapeless, unrooted to time and reality, a cluster of darkly lit monuments spied from the back seat of a car, I assured her that, yes, it was.

• • •

There's one landmark I remember clearly from that night: Auguste Rodin's sculpture garden. Through the iron fence, the garden seemed almost wild, filled with silhouettes of roses and pompom-like flowers, statues rising out of the tall grass, slender and pensive, with smooth, bronze-dark faces, and garments permanently windblown. There was the thinker, and there, the unfinished gates of hell. The museum was closed, of course — by now, it was well past one in the morning — so I pressed myself against the fence, absorbing as much as I could of the half-hidden statues, which, though giant and stylized, seemed so lifelike that I thought they might descend their pedestals and meet me at the museum gates. I promised myself I'd return someday.

• • •

In 1902, the poet Rainer Maria Rilke also travelled to Paris to see Auguste Rodin's sculptures. He'd hoped to write a book about the master sculptor but instead found himself working as Rodin's secretary, organizing his files and managing his correspondence so that Rodin could work on his art. Rilke wasn't writing a lot of poetry at the time, but with Rodin's encouragement, he began visiting art museums and the local zoo nearly every day. This was for creative inspiration. The artist "must work, always work," Rodin told him, if he was to produce anything of value. He must make a habit of creating.

Rodin's instruction transformed Rilke from a poet who waited for inspiration to one who pushed everything aside to make room for it. Rilke began to write every day. He even wrote a poem about this shift in his perspective. In the poem, the speaker encounters the archaic marble torso of Apollo. Awestruck, he sees his world for its smallness and ordinariness and decides then and there: "You must change your life."[1] One can almost hear Rodin's voice speaking through the stone.

For better or for worse, Rilke came to share his employer's belief that the artist's vocation was supreme: No relationship, commitment, or family obligation should get in the way of the work. The art must always come first. The relationship between the temperamental Rodin and his ambitious assistant ended acrimoniously, though. When Rilke quit his administrative position to become a full-time poet, the sculptor had to find a new secretary.

• • •

Looking back on this account of artistic mentorship, I realize that Rodin's advice to Rilke was to become what is now called an "art monster": the artist who puts work above everything and everyone. The writer Jenny Offill popularized the term in her novel *Dept. of Speculation*. The novel is told from the point of view of a writer who can't throw off her everyday responsibilities but still wants to dedicate her life to her craft.[2] She uses the example of the Russian-American novelist Vladimir Nabokov and his wife, Véra, to consider her predicament: "My plan was to never get married. I was going to be an art monster instead. Women almost never become art monsters because art monsters only concern themselves with art, never mundane things. Nabokov didn't even fold his own umbrella. Vera licked his stamps for him."[3]

It's true. The single-mindedness, the unstoppable drive, the belief in the work above all else — these are characteristics often aligned with solitary male geniuses such as Nabokov, Rodin, Rilke, or Picasso. Was there a female equivalent?

Rachel Cusk tackles the question of whether there's a female counterpart to the male art monster in an essay entitled "Can a Woman Who Is an Artist Ever Just Be an Artist?" The essay examines the Picasso-like figure of the historical male artist who "does everything we are told not to do: He is violent and selfish. He neglects or betrays his friends and family. He smokes, drinks, scandalizes, indulges his lusts and in every way bites the hand that feeds him, all to be unmasked at the end as a peerless genius." He does the things, Cusk writes, that we're least able or least willing to do: "to work without expectation of a reward, to dispense with material comfort and to maintain an absolute indifference to what other people think of him. For he is the intimate associate of beauty and the world's truth, dispenser of that rare substance — art — by which we are capable of feeling our lives to be elevated." He is treated as a vessel, channelling the divine spark of genius, and so he's exonerated. But historically this hasn't been the same for the woman artist. The double standard still persists. Cusk ultimately asks: "Today when a female artist sets out to create, who is she?"[4] Should she strive to become an art monster or something new entirely?

Lauren Elkin points out that there are some woman art monsters. But she also notes that mothers who became art monsters historically did so by leaving or harming their children through abandonment like Doris Lessing, through suicide like Sylvia Plath, or through abuse like Anne Sexton. Or, as we have seen, through silence, like Alice Munro.

There's also the case of the artist who becomes monstrous from *not* creating. Virginia Woolf writes about that monstrousness in *A Room of One's Own*: "When, however, one reads of a witch being ducked, of a woman possessed by devils, of a wise woman selling herbs ... we are on the track of a lost novelist, a suppressed poet, of some mute and inglorious Jane Austen, some Emily Brontë who dashed her brains out on the moor or mopped and mowed about the highways crazed with the torture that her gift had put her to."[5] Toni Morrison writes of this monstrous figure in a description of her character, Sula, the pariah on the outskirts of town — "like an artist with no art form, she became dangerous."[6] In these cases, the thwarted woman artist is poisoned by her own ambition. She is deemed frightening.

But there were some exceptions to this model. One writer who managed to sidestep the fate of the thwarted woman artist and join the ranks of undisputed genius shared by Nabokov, Rodin, Rilke, and Picasso was Gertrude Stein.

The high priestess of the early twentieth-century modernist art movement lived most of her life in Montmartre, not far from where I'd stayed on my brief sojourn to Paris. My hosts hadn't stopped at 27 rue de Fleurus on our midnight tour, though, and even if they had, I would have been too tired to get out of the car. I'd have to find another way to visit her Saturday night salon — the room where careers were made and genius was born.

2

The experimental poet Gertrude Stein and the experimental painter Pablo Picasso were friends for a time in Paris as the twentieth-century art canon was still forming, like the parts of a baby's skull coalescing after birth. It was a good time to be in Paris and to be rich or know someone who was both those things, which was partly the basis of Picasso and Stein's friendship.

Stein was born to a wealthy family in Pennsylvania and raised in Oakland, California, where her father was the director of San Francisco's streetcar lines. She pursued a bachelor of arts at Radcliffe College, then part of Harvard University, where she researched and experimented with automatic writing: a practice said to be produced by a spiritual or subconscious agency rather than by the conscious intention of the writer. Next came a stint in medical school at Johns Hopkins University where, much to the dismay of her former adviser who claimed Stein was his "most brilliant woman student," she apparently grew bored with her studies and dropped out.

At least boredom was the reason she gave. Was it boredom or the stress of studying a male-dominated profession in a deeply paternalistic culture? Perhaps both. Or maybe it was due to unrequited love. For while at Johns Hopkins, Stein formed a crush on the political activist Mary Bookstaver, who was already involved in a relationship with another female medical student. Whatever the reason — boredom, patriarchy, or heartbreak — Stein had had enough of America.[7] In 1903, she moved to Paris, where she lived for the rest of her life and where she hosted her famous literary salons at 27 rue de Fleurus, not far from where Rodin carved sculptures while Rilke kept his books.

It's hard to imagine entering Stein's salon, though I've tried by obsessively reading the authors and poets who passed through its doors, and by watching *Midnight in Paris*, the 2011 fantasy film by Woody Allen — another particularly monstrous art monster.[8] This movie is memorable to me because of its lush depiction of Gertrude Stein's living room — this was pretty much the main reason I watched the film — but also its message. As Allen's time traveller, the aspiring American novelist Gil Pender, played by Owen Wilson, haphazardly bumps into a succession of the famous, and also mostly male, artists and writers of 1920s Paris (Ernest Hemingway, Georges Braque, Pablo Picasso, F. Scott Fitzgerald, Salvador Dalí), he notices a general sense of dissatisfaction. It turns out that these artists yearn for a supposedly simpler, more passionate, earlier time. When Gil accidentally travels farther back in time to the Belle Époque of the late 1800s with Picasso's mistress and muse, Adriana, the fictional composite of Fernande Olivier and Marie-Thérèse Walter, they encounter Henri de Toulouse-Lautrec, Paul Gauguin, and Edgar Degas in the Moulin Rouge, who all agree that the Renaissance was the best era. Gil leaves Adriana in the 1890s where Gauguin already appears to be moving in to seduce her. The film's message is clear: No generation is aware of their time when they're living it; each generation romanticizes earlier eras and earlier figures of genius.

• • •

The moment of time into which we're born and spend our formative years can feel saturated with a sense of belatedness, of being outside history, or removed from it. This was the case for me, coming of age in the Y2K era, and the case for many people I knew growing up. In fact, I remember a friend I made in university lamenting how everything fun and revolutionary had already happened decades before our births and without our participation in it. What he'd give to go back to the 1960s! He conjured up Woodstock's bell-bottomed crowds listening to Janis Joplin, preaching free love, and hugging in the rain. For an affable middle-class white man — like Gil Pender in *Midnight in Paris,* and like my university friend who wished to return to the 1960s — time travel would be a romp.

"Wouldn't it be great?" my friend asked. "The world was so much more alive then."

"Perhaps for some," I said. I didn't remind him that in the 1960s there was still a 50 percent wage gap between men and women.

I can imagine decades from now another young person trying to picture the early days of the internet and that pre-digital innocence when children still played outdoors. The sense of possibility: the whole world breaking open, its social geography shrinking, its communities expanding through the invisible Web. In this future, there will most certainly be another boyish university student leaning into his companion's ear and musing, *What would you give to go back to the 1990s?* And his companion might think: *Low-rise jeans, heroin chic–inspired eating disorders. No one out of the closet in high school. No thanks.*

The British neurologist Oliver Sacks noted that the memory changes every time it's accessed, meaning that it's never in the past but is actually a thought process undertaken in the perpetual present. In other words, to remember isn't only to return to a memory but to re-create it. This is the case with our cultural memory as well: We remake our histories through the act of remembering. I remember having this conversation with my university friend on a beach during summer vacation. But maybe it was simply an email exchange and I've rewritten the memory to include the beach, and now this beach, with its white sand and glacial waters, is so fixed in my mind I can't dislodge it from my memory of the conversation. Now when I return to this memory, I question whether we were friends at all. Perhaps this would-be time traveller wasn't a pal but a boy I wanted to impress, and so when he expressed his desire to go back to the 1960s, I'd agreed to go with him. Yes, we'd jump through the ice-green waters of the lake into another time.

• • •

I don't miss what I remember of the 1990s, or my teenage years in the early 2000s, but like Gil Pender, I still fall prey to an inherited bout of nostalgia for 27 rue de Fleurus. Maybe this is why I've continued to search for the sense of artistic community the salon seems to have offered its guests. This was, after all, why I'd moved to Berlin, which was a kind of grungy cousin to Paris and was, during this time, affordable, unruly, sleepless, alive. "Poor but sexy" was the slogan scrawled in English on the side of a tall building in Friedrichshain where I briefly worked as a cupcake baker in a cupcake café. This is also why I keep asking: What are the conditions for an artistic community? And does a person need one in order to create art? But it was more complicated than that, I realized. There was the question of membership. Who was welcome in this community — who had traditionally been welcomed?

What if, in Gil's place, I was to travel back to 1920s Paris and knock on the door of Gertrude Stein's salon. Alice B. Toklas might greet me on the threshold, look me over with curiosity or mistrust — I hope curiosity. She is tall and slight, bewhiskered, with a long, intelligent face. If I'm invited in, I'll follow Toklas into a room filled with heavy wooden furniture. Canvases cover every inch of wall space, like a quilt, the great quilt of modernist art. But I don't have time to identify each painting because I feel a hand on my elbow. A voice asks me if I'm lost or if I'm someone's wife. This must be Ernest Hemingway. He's smiling at me encouragingly, brown eyes flickering with interest, but there's something else in his face, an unmistakable hostility I'll only recognize later when I tell him I, too, am a writer. I know this look. It belongs to a man who believes women can't make art, not really — not seriously.

Will Hemingway steer me to Gertrude Stein, the exception in his mind? Her imperial figure at the hearth magnetizes the salon. She's the true north of every room she enters. By her side stands the youthful Spanish prodigy, thin and dark, with big pools for eyes, listening with intensity to his benefactor. Stein will later describe Picasso as "violent," though not "rough."[9]

I've read that Stein was deeply curious about everyone who came across her path, and I can feel this curiosity radiating from her broad open face, which now turns toward me like the sun. I must find a way to impress her.

Before I can speak, I feel the gentle but firm hand on my elbow once again as Hemingway leads me to the back of the room where the wives and mistresses sit. They turn their collective face upon me.

There's Amélie Matisse, *femme d'intérieur*, dark hair heaped on her head as in her portrait with the green line down her nose. Beside her, the Madonna-like Alice Princet, newly Alice Derain, married to the brooding André Derain, whose hooked gaze seeks her out. Next, Germaine Pichot, who has "the square shoulders and the unseeing fixed eyes of a Spanish woman."[10] At the head of the table sits the solemn and beautiful Fernande Olivier, first muse of Picasso and model for many artists on the Left Bank. Fernande Olivier is an artist as well, but a woman can't be both an artist and a muse. Not at this time in history. Even Stein drew a sharp distinction between "geniuses" and the "wives of geniuses," assigning Alice to sit "very often and very long with many wives and wives of many geniuses."[11]

There's one writer I'm desperate to meet, but I won't find her here. She also lived in Paris in the early twentieth century, but though she was one of the most brilliant and formally innovative novelists of her time, she was a perpetual outsider to the literary community. Most likely, I'd find her in a bar on the West Bank.

I'm referring to the West Indies–born literary genius Jean Rhys. Her sentences drill inward in an exercise in ruthless self-exploration. At the same time, they feel like mirrors, fragmented shards through which I catch my own reflection, my own fear and frustration. They're unlike anything I've read before.

I look around the room, but Jean Rhys isn't here.

As I take a seat at the wives' table, I can feel Stein's observant eye, missing nothing. Stein, too, is interested in stories told from the outside — stories told by women. But in this moment in time, her central project is to cultivate, alongside Pablo Picasso, her reputation as a genius.

• • •

Gertrude Stein's obsession with genius could stem from the fact that she didn't feel she was taken seriously as a writer. Stein's brother, Leo, who was resentful of his sister after Alice B. Toklas displaced him as her confidant, didn't like or respect Stein's writing. Leo believed she wrote the way she did because she couldn't write proper English. He also believed that it wasn't her writing, but her persona, her patronage in the art world, that had brought her acclaim. "He said it was not it it was I," Stein writes in her circuitous way.[12] "If I was not there to be there with what I did then what I did would not be what it was." She adds: "It did not trouble me." But it did.

Along with the self-appointed title of genius, Stein claimed in art-monsterish fashion — perhaps with tongue in cheek — that she possessed a singular talent. Of herself, in third person, Stein wrote: "In English literature in her time she is the only one."

Stein was writing at the same time as Jean Rhys, Nella Larsen, James Joyce, Virginia Woolf, and F. Scott Fitzgerald, but that didn't matter to her: She was the only one.

• • •

I admire Stein for her insistence on being recognized as a genius. Her determination recalls something the American painter Georgia O'Keeffe once said: "Men put me down as the best woman painter. I think I'm one of the best painters." Both were bold claims for a woman to make in the early twentieth century.

What does it mean, though, to think of yourself as the only one? It requires an astonishing confidence in your work.

It seems to me that to be the only one is to be, above all else, the only one advocating for your art. It is to demand a room of your own, and to be the only one in the room. It is to close the door and not ask permission to do so. It is to believe your work is worth defending against everyone rattling the doorknob.

Stein had help with this defence of her privacy, though. Toklas guarded her study door.

3

In the post-#MeToo twenty-first century, the cultural celebration of the art monster seems to be fading. The fact is few of us have a partner who will fold our umbrellas, lick our stamps, or return our Amazon packages for us, who will take over the mundane activities of daily life, what the poet Bernadette Mayer calls the "formidable ordinary order" of the day so that the art monster can exist at all.[13] More people, it seems to me, are asking: Is there instead a way to live as a hybrid creature, part artist, part decent human being?

But in the early twentieth century, when Rilke first visited Rodin, when Picasso first arrived in Paris with a suitcase and a box of paints, when Gertrude Stein first opened the doors to her salon, the figure of the art monster was alive and well. Not only that, the art monster was indistinguishable from the figure of the genius.

I'd once romanticized the writers and artists who frequented Stein's salon. But the more I learned about the artists whose paintings covered its walls, the more skeptical I became of the project of genius-making. Was the title of Next Picasso even a welcome one? I mean, beyond the high school gimmick. I wasn't so sure anymore.

I pressed deeper, but this only yielded darker and more disturbing discoveries.

• • •

Gertrude Stein and Pablo Picasso first met at the Salon d'Automne in Paris in 1905 because of a painting. It was one of Picasso's early works, now one of the most expensive artworks in the world. At first, Stein didn't want to buy it. She could recognize the artist's talent, but something about the painting "repelled and shocked her … she did not want it in the house."[14] She and her brother, Leo, argued over its purchase; in the end, Leo had his way and they acquired their first Picasso.

I was curious what this painting looked like — this picture that had first repulsed Stein but then had prompted her iconic friendship with and patronage of Picasso, a companionship that would confirm Paris as the modernist mecca for art and literature.

The painting *Fillette nue au panier de fleurs* depicts a pale, prepubescent child standing awkwardly against a blue background, a basket of red flowers in her hands. Save for a pink ribbon in her dark hair and a double string of pearls around her neck, she's naked. She has the body of a child, but her face, staring out from the painting at an angle, is the face of a much older woman. Her pupils are solid black. There's a line of crimson on her lips. Sharp, knowing, she hooks eyes with the viewer. Her look is resigned, tired, as if to say, "Oh, you again."

The model was a Parisian street girl named Linda (which comes from the Spanish word meaning "pretty," so it might have simply been a nickname) who worked as a flower seller in the Montmartre district where Picasso lived. It's likely she also worked as a child prostitute. This painting sold at Christie's in 2018 for US$115 million.

I can't stop staring at Linda's face, her listless expression. It's difficult to meet her still, black eyes.

• • •

Two years after he sold Linda's portrait to the Steins, Picasso and his long-term mistress, Fernande Olivier, decided to adopt a child from the local orphanage. Olivier was unable to bear children but desperately wanted a child. Her and Picasso's relationship was often volatile and even violent, and she felt that a child would give them stability and make them feel more like a family. They adopted thirteen-year-old Raymonde, who came to live with them in Montmartre. But this small family only lasted four months. The story goes that one day Olivier came home to find amongst Picasso's drawings a nude sketch of the girl, which the artist had titled *Raymonde Examining Her Foot.* Olivier immediately sent her adopted daughter back to the orphanage.[15]

Some have suggested that Fernande Olivier saw Raymonde as a rival for Picasso's affection, and that was why she sent her away. Others believe that Olivier knew what Picasso, the art monster, was capable of. She was protecting the child from a predatory man.[16]

Picasso's name is now synonymous with artistic genius. But what or who was sacrificed to furnish him with this title? At the bottom of so many of these accounts of artist and muse is a story of a harmed child.

• • •

Linda's portrait reminds me of another disturbing image: a photograph taken by realist painter and photographer Thomas Eakins of a young unnamed Black girl in Philadelphia in the late nineteenth century. The photograph features a naked child on a dusty arabesque sofa in Eakins's attic studio. She gazes flatly at the camera, her hand curled stiffly under her chin. She can't be more than nine or ten years old.

As with Picasso's painting of the Parisian flower seller, it's hard to meet the child's stare. There's something so resigned, so abject and unsettling about her expression, that the act of looking feels like a violation. The viewer is filled with shame.

There's little trace of this unnamed girl beyond Eakins's photograph. No record in the Philadelphia archives and public accounts. Photographs of the tenement where this young girl lived appear in a police brief and a charity report, but she's barely visible peering out of the third-floor window.

Of the child in the photograph, the critic Saidiya Hartman writes: "The girl's gaze says everything about the kind of female property she is — one not in the class of those deserving protection." Without a name, she becomes a placeholder for the possibilities and the dangers awaiting Black girls and women in that era, when people of colour had few rights and the age of consent was ten years old. "The minor figure yields to the chorus," writes Hartman. "All their hurt and promise are hers to bear."[17]

These girls and women gaze out of a muted past, but their gaze doesn't strike me as silent. From the pink sands of Tahiti, the dilapidated artists' studios of Montmartre, or the abject attic in Philadelphia, these figures stare out of the picture frames, past the artist, with gazes that resist silence. Theirs is a loud stare.

4

Almost Genius

1

LONDON, 1797. MARY WOLLSTONECRAFT, MOTHER OF FEMinist thought in England, lies in the throes of a three-day-long fever. This fever, so common in the eighteenth century it was called "childbed fever," is caused by an infection when the placenta ruptures during birth.[1] The baby is healthy. She will be named Mary after her mother and will eventually go on to write *Frankenstein*, another story about a monstrous birth.

I've fantasized about dropping back in time — not to Gertrude Stein's salon this time but farther back to Wollstonecraft's bedside where hour by hour life is seeping away. *Maria: Or, the Wrongs of Woman*, the sequel to *A Vindication of the Rights of Woman*, sits on her bedside table unfinished. The manuscript is a novel about a woman imprisoned in an insane asylum by her husband. Earlier that year, Wollstonecraft visited Bethlem Royal Hospital (a.k.a. Bedlam) to research the book.

After administrating a dose of penicillin to Wollstonecraft, I'd travel to 1855 Yorkshire to look in on Charlotte Brontë, who is suffering from hyperemesis gravidarum, a severe form of so-called morning sickness, which leaves its victims fatally dehydrated, malnourished, and vomiting blood-streaked bile.[2] On her last morning, Charlotte surfaced from her delirium, and in a moment of clarity, turned to her husband in disbelief: "Oh, I am not going to die, am I? He will not separate us." She had just begun writing another book, *Emma*.

If only I could hook Charlotte up to an IV and nurse her back to health. If only I could yell at Mary's doctors to wash their hands. What work would these authors have produced — what ideas, novels, poems, and manifestos, what material changes to women's lives might they have accelerated had they lived past thirty-eight?

• • •

"A woman writer," in Virginia Woolf's words, must "think back through her mothers" in order to create art. We must think back through what Maggie Nelson calls the "many-gendered mothers of the heart."[3] Or, in Alice Walker's formulation, by way of the poem by Marilou Awiakta, the nurturing "Motheroot."[4] By thinking back or writing back through our literary ancestors, we keep them alive. Bernadette Mayer frames this communion with a literary matriarchy a little differently. She writes:

> There are certain dead writers
> who are like mothers who are more like moths
> coming to the light at night like friends[5]

Here the many-gendered literary mothers and grandmothers take on a shifting, glimmering expression — winged presences circling the mind's lamp, drawing close to imagination's flare. Whether the woman writer drops back in time to think back through her mothers, or whether those literary mothers flutter into the present in animal guise, the idea is the same: A writer is never writing alone. Genius isn't born in isolation.

Many of my own literary mothers weren't themselves biological mothers. Pregnancy was, until recently in many parts of the world, an extremely hazardous occupation, as we see with Charlotte Brontë and Mary Wollstonecraft, who both died of childbirth-related causes at the prime of their writing careers. Even if the eighteenth- or nineteenth-century women artists survived childbirth, the challenges only continued after at an unrelenting pace.

This was the case for the celebrated nineteenth-century Southern U.S. author Kate Chopin. She was raised by her mother, grandmother, and great-grandmother, her father having died in a bridge collapse when she was very young. History repeated itself when Chopin's husband died of malaria, leaving her with six children and US$42,000 in debt, the equivalent of approximately US$1.33 million in 2024.

I'm drawn to Chopin's story because my family suffered a similar fate. My grandfather — my mother's father — died young of a heart attack in the middle of the night. He left behind eight children, my mother the youngest at sixteen months. I can't imagine what it must have been like for my grandmother to be responsible for eight children and a farm, now suddenly on her own. Her church suggested that she keep the oldest four children, who would be able to help out on the farm, and give the younger four up for adoption. She refused. Instead, she sold pieces of the farm, determined to keep the family together.

Chopin didn't give up hope, either. Having been raised in a family of smart, independent women, she found her footing. Now a single mother of six children all under nine years old, Chopin turned to writing to support her family, publishing short stories and articles in periodicals and magazines. This seemed to work out for her until she published *The Awakening*, the novel that effectively ended her writing career.[6] Set in nineteenth-century New Orleans, *The Awakening* explores the sexual and artistic awakening of young wife and mother Edna Pontellier, who abandons her family in the hope of finding an alternative way to live. Edna doesn't discover a viable alternative, and even though she's just learned how to swim, commits suicide by walking into the sea. In fact, it was the water scenes that most captivated me when I read the novel — the possibility and danger of this sensual, all-prevailing element. One line strikes me in particular: "She turned her face seaward to gather in an impression of space and solitude."[7]

I picture Chopin at her writing desk trying to revise her novel as her toddler and baby play at her feet, her daughter braids her hair, and her sons argue for custody of her lap. No wonder she wrote about ambivalent motherhood and wifehood, of female independence and desire. Through the voice of her protagonist, Edna, we hear Chopin: "I would give up the unessential; I would give up my money, I would give up my life for my children; but I wouldn't give myself. I can't make it more clear; it's only something I am beginning to comprehend, which is revealing itself to me."[8]

Chopin didn't write another novel, though she did continue to produce stories but had difficulty publishing them.[9]

Only after her death did critics come to appreciate Chopin's work, noting, as reviewer Fred Lewis Pattee did in 1915, that she displayed "what may be described as a native aptitude for narration amounting almost to genius."[10] (Trust an early twentieth-century male critic to use the phrase "amounting almost to genius," even when applauding a female author.) *The Awakening* is now considered one of the greatest works of American literature. Like Jean Rhys, like Mary Wollstonecraft, the "almost genius" Chopin was writing for a future audience, her ideas too radical for her time. In Ralph Waldo Emerson's words, "Genius always finds itself a century too early."

2

The word *genius* comes from the Latin *gignere* for "beget" or "to give birth or bring forth." *Gignere* evolved into the Middle English *genius*, defined as a "guardian deity or spirit that watches over each person from birth." Over the following centuries, the term's meaning shifted to describe "a person's characteristic disposition" or "natural ability," which led to "a person's exceptional natural ability." The word *genius* also originates from the Latin for "the male spirit of a gens" — *gens* being a paternal line with the members having a common name and worshipping a common ancestor. So, though the word holds within it the act of giving birth, it takes on a male association — a self-generating patrilineal clan. Think Athena, goddess of war and wisdom, bypassing the maternal and springing fully formed from the head of Zeus, her father. The father is the artist. The daughter, his creation. The binary extends to man = artist. Woman = art.

Initially, people who displayed remarkable talent were referred to as "having a genius" — as in having a genius for portrait painting or lute carving — but as the concept evolved, *genius* was applied to the person who displayed the talent. It was only in the eighteenth century that the term began to resemble the way we use it now, so that as well as talking about people "having a genius" you could also talk about them "being a genius."

Tracking the etymology and evolution of the term in her book *Gender and Genius*, Christine Battersby describes how Renaissance women were believed to lack genius because of a deficiency in what was known as the *ingenium* — those inherited mental and physical talents that helped artists conceive and execute their projects. Due to their biology, women, apparently, were fated to lack wit, judgment, and skill, and so cultural inferiority became linked with femaleness. "Even in the Renaissance," Battersby writes, "what made a human being great was what made him distinctively *not-female.* There is nothing accidental about the way that the Romantic concept of genius is gendered: the term was forged at the point where two modes of misogyny meet.... The creative and the procreative."[11]

Why were men biologically predisposed to genius and women not? According to the medical beliefs of the Renaissance, the "fibres" of the female body were not "elastic" enough to withstand the rigours of genius. The theory of the bodily humours characterized male bodies as "hot and dry" but female bodies as "cold and moist," and the vapours that arise from the uterus, it was believed, clouded the mind and dimmed the ability to apprehend "Truth."[12] The great artist was one who could transcend reason by a kind of fiery "madness," breaking away temporarily from ordinary human limitations, but due to her wet and cloudy anatomy, a woman wasn't able to physically participate in this act of transcendence.[13]

In the eighteenth century, as the Age of Enlightenment waned, thinkers no longer accepted that reason alone distinguished man from animal. There was a renewed interest in the idea of creativity as a distinguishing human feature and an almost godly trait. From the eighteenth century and on into the nineteenth century, Europe became obsessed with the concept of genius. A new language of exclusion emerged: Man was already superior to animals, but now he found a way to articulate himself as superior to other human beings — Indigenous Peoples and women, for example. Genius came to mean a particular individual who is specially endowed with the "divine spark" of creativity. I'm reminded of God bestowing on Adam the touch of life in Michelangelo's fresco, and of Mary Shelley's Dr. Frankenstein giving life to his monster — a genius scientist playing God. Or of Nathaniel Hawthorne's Dr. Rappaccini, another mad scientist character who, to protect his daughter's chastity, transforms her into a cyborg-like creature, poisonous to the touch.

The investment in this concept of a transcendent male genius in the eighteenth and nineteenth centuries was also partly due to the emerging debates surrounding women's social roles and intellectual and creative capacities. It simply became more difficult to unquestionably assume the inferiority of women's intellect compared to men's when reading Emily Brontë or Jane Austen, or when listening to the speeches of Mary Wollstonecraft or abolitionist Sojourner Truth. New branding was needed to maintain male intellectual dominance, and separate male writers from what Hawthorne in 1855 called the "damned mob of scribbling women." Hawthorne made this comment when complaining to his publisher that women writers had taken over the literary scene and were weakening his chances at publication and of reaching a larger audience. "America is now wholly given over to a damned mob of scribbling women, and I should have no chance of success," he lamented.[14] It was these kinds of fears that lead to genius being remodelled as an inherently (white) male capacity. As a result, the idea of genius became a tool to exclude women from serious creative and intellectual activity. This continues all the way up to the present when a monument to one woman's intellectual success is refused a place in a square full of statues of men. At the same time, this obsessive protection of male genius also reveals to us how historically the categories of artist and muse were beginning to be questioned, how they were beginning to shift.

The American poet Emily Dickinson was interested in this shift. Of women's exclusion from the nineteenth-century literary sphere, she wrote:

> They shut me up in Prose —
> As when a little Girl
> They put me in the Closet —
> Because they liked me "still" —
>
> Still! Could themself have peeped —
> And seen my Brain — go round —
> They might as wise have lodged a Bird
> For Treason — in the Pound —[15]

Dickinson points out how language can be used to "shut up" and punish women writers, treating them like little girls who need to be locked in a closet to learn how to be "still" — here, meaning both passive and quiet. Dickinson repeats the word *still* in the next stanza, this time with an exclamation point, to emphasize another meaning of the word: *nevertheless*. "Still," she writes, if these literary gatekeepers could see "my Brain — go round" they might realize they haven't successfully quieted the female poet at all. In fact, their attempt to constrain the poet's voice was as foolish as trying to imprison "a Bird / For Treason — in the Pound": to confine a bird that can easily escape through the prison bars.

Language, Dickinson shows us, is a slippery medium. It can be used to regulate and discipline, but it can also be turned back on itself to create new meanings.

3

When I was a graduate student, I met a Ph.D. candidate at a local conference, a young man finishing up a thesis on Ezra Pound, who asked me what I was writing about.

"Broad strokes," he said affably, as he knew as well as I that no doctoral student likes to discuss their dissertation-in-progress, especially when they haven't yet hit upon an argument and are too busy taking on part-time teaching contracts to actually spend any time with the project.

"I'm writing about contemporary women writers," I told him.

"Oh," he said, "are there any?" He thought for a moment and then nodded. "I guess there's J.K. Rowling."

I thought he was joking at first, but he wasn't.

"I love *Harry Potter*," he said.

I don't consider Rowling representative of contemporary women writers, and I find her views on gender transphobic, but the fact that she's the only writer this Ph.D. candidate could name is meaningful. My colleague was what I dubbed "the Netflix and Milton" variety of grad student — the kind of scholar dedicated to exploring a single author or narrow aspect of literary history, the years 1667–68, for example, and spending the rest of the time watching *The Avengers* or *The Big Bang Theory*, oblivious to the rhythms of the current literary landscape. To be clear, there's nothing wrong with this — I've done it myself at times (who hasn't?) — but still, I was surprised by the limit of my colleague's curiosity. But then, can you be curious about something you don't know exists? Maybe this lack of curiosity was more pervasive than I initially realized, especially when it came to women's intellect and artistic prowess.

Even now, as I write this, the question of whether a female genius exists is still very much a live one. The questions Mary Wollstonecraft was grappling with in 1792 in *A Vindication of the Rights of Woman* and the questions Virginia Woolf contends with in *A Room of One's Own* still endure. As we see in the art historian Linda Nochlin's provocatively titled 1970s essay "Why Have There Been No Great Women Artists?" — the essay itself a response to the glib question put to Nochlin by a male gallerist — these questions do more than endure. They shape a culture. Examining how women artists were hobbled by institutional strictures and social prejudices, Nochlin writes: "The fault lies not in the stars, our hormones, our menstrual cycles, or our empty internal spaces, but in our institutions and our education — education understood to include everything that happens to us from the moment we enter this world of meaningful symbols, signs, and signals."[16] In other words, the idea that women aren't capable of greatness has (until recently) been part of our social education from a very young age.

Even Simone de Beauvoir refused to see women as geniuses. In *The Second Sex*, a book that's said to mark the beginning of second-wave feminism across the globe, Beauvoir writes: "There are women who are mad and there are women of talent: none has that madness in her talent that we call genius." She does concede that this is mostly to do with social conditions: "One is not born a genius, one becomes a genius," she reflects, "and the feminine situation has up to the present rendered this becoming practically impossible." Women, Beauvoir continues, have contributed to "a literature of protest" with their "sincere and powerful works," but they lack "irony," "ease," "calm sincerity," and "abstract elegance." This sounds very similar to the Renaissance ideas of women's bodies being too damp to inspire the spark of genius.[17]

I recognize the sentiment even today. This is not to say that nowadays the majority of people dismiss the notion that female genius exists — we assume it must exist; it must, right? — but rather that if you bring up the subject of artistic female genius at a party, whoever you're talking to will think for a moment, a small, anxious frown furrowing the brow, and then begin to name artists who might fit this category. But each name will be offered with a question, suggesting uncertainty or even dismissiveness. Sylvia Plath? Frida Kahlo?

A brief Google search for "female genius" reflects this ambivalence in its results:

> Are there female geniuses?
> Can intelligence be feminine?
> Who is the most genius woman?

This sense of uncertainty isn't present when the situation is reversed and one is discussing male geniuses, or simply, genius. Shakespeare, Beethoven, David Foster Wallace, your party conversationalist will reply. Or Michelangelo, Leonardo da Vinci. As Megan Garber observes in *The Atlantic*, "Guess who the first season of that new show *Genius* is about? I'll give you a hint: The first name of the genius in question is Albert. The subject of the show's second season? Pablo."[18]

Given its patriarchal history, some have argued we should get rid of the term *genius* altogether. In 2017, several U.K. news outlets debated Cambridge University's initiative to move away from using terms like *genius*, *flair*, and *brilliance* in assessment, since these terms were deemed to still be associated with men. Was it possible to inject the term with new meaning? Could the term *genius* be amended and widened to be more inclusive — like the square in Padua? Perhaps a more useful question is: What can the history of this word tell us about the history of women's creativity and resourcefulness?

What was coming to light as I tunnelled down the history of genius — and the underexplored history of female genius — was just how malleable, how subjective, the concept of genius is. Like the modernist period, like our own period, this concept is also soft-skulled and developing, unfixed.

• • •

In her 2004 article "Is There a Feminine Genius?" philosopher and psychoanalyst Julia Kristeva argues that being labelled a "genius" means being regarded as unique, and more significantly, as embodying "the most complex, the most appealing, and the most fruitful form of this uniqueness at a particular moment in history." It involves possessing an exceptional quality that's "lasting and universal." But she also finds the term *genius* a little embarrassing. She sees it as hyperbolic and seems reluctant to use it to describe women artists and thinkers, even trailblazers such as Simone de Beauvoir, Hannah Arendt, and Colette. Kristeva is skeptical of the idea of a distinct, essential "feminine genius" that might counterbalance the dominant masculine model and argues that women's individuality and diverse experiences can't — and shouldn't — be reduced to a singular concept of feminine genius.

Instead, Kristeva calls for a more fluid, pluralistic understanding of creativity and intellectual contribution that transcends gender. Genius, she writes, "is quite simply creativity." But she also adds: "You are a genius to the extent that you are able to challenge the sociohistorical conditions of your identity." In other words, her argument's logic is circular: Genius should simply be about creativity full stop. But the socio-economic and historical contexts exist, too. So maybe genius isn't exclusively about creativity because creativity can't be separated from its context.[19]

It would be so much simpler if we could dispense with the socio-historical circumstances of genius, but we can't. There are material conditions to having the time to think and write and create, and these get bound up in gender expectations due to the systems we live in.

Virginia Woolf provides an example of this impossibility to separate genius from its socio-historical context through the invented case of Judith Shakespeare. Judith Shakespeare is William Shakespeare's imagined twin sister who shares his incandescent mind and voracious talent, but who, because of her gender, is unable to realize her genius.

While William goes off to grammar school to learn Latin and read Ovid, Virgil, and Horace, his extraordinarily gifted sister remains at home, as was the tradition for girls. Judith might have been as adventurous and imaginative as her brother, but she has no chance to learn grammar and logic, let alone read Virgil. If she manages to pen a few pages on the sly, she's careful to hide or destroy them. Resisting an arranged marriage, Judith runs away to London — the "force of her own gift alone drove her to it."

Although she's talented and hopes to become an actor and playwright, in London she faces ridicule and lechery. "Men laughed in her face … bellowed something about poodles dancing and women acting — no woman … could possibly be an actress.… She could get no training in her craft. Could she even seek her dinner in a tavern or roam the streets at midnight? Yet her genius was for fiction and lusted to feed abundantly upon the lives of men and women and the study of their ways."

Eventually, she attracts the attention of a sleazy theatre manager, but not the kind of attention she was hoping for, the kind to advance her career. (How familiar this sounds and how often repeated in our own twenty-first-century institutions.) The story ends abruptly and tragically:

> She found herself with child by that gentleman and so — who shall measure the heat and violence of the poet's heart when caught and tangled in a woman's body? — killed herself one winter's night and lies buried at some cross-roads where the omnibuses now stop outside the Elephant and Castle.

This, Woolf contends, is more or less how the story would run if a woman in Shakespeare's day had had Shakespeare's genius.[20] Woolf ends on a hopeful note, though, by suggesting that female genius is not confined to physical writings or public recognition. "Now my belief is that this poet who never wrote a word and was buried at the cross-roads still lives," Woolf assures her audience:

> She lives in you and in me, and in many other women who are not here tonight, for they are washing up the dishes and putting the children to bed. But she lives, for great poets do not die; they are continuing presences; they need only the opportunity to walk among us in the flesh.[21]

"She lives in you and in me." It was this sentiment that gave me — and many other writers I've spoken with — the sense of permission to even consider the pursuit of a creative life. The permission to shut the door.

This idea of self-permission reminds me of another Woolf character — her sinister trad wife, the Angel in the House, who stands for female purity, subservience, and wholesomeness, and who pressures the woman writer to only write nice, polite things. Assassinating the angel, Woolf believed, was part of the occupation of a woman writer, if she hoped to be any good. The angel must die for Judith to live. She must die for a woman artist to obtain the habit of freedom. Or, in the words of Leonora Carrington, she "must be devoured."[22]

• • •

After my encounter with the Ph.D. candidate who didn't read books by women, I returned to the university library whose stacks housed so many of those "almost genius" literary mothers. This was where I spent most of my day, beneath its brutalist columns, hunched over a laptop. This particular evening was no different, but I felt restless. As the sun dropped behind the skyscrapers, I cast a backward glance over my life.

Had I ever really allowed myself permission to think of myself as an artist? I glimpsed the awkward high school art student, the childminder in Berlin, now the graduate student, so unprotective of her time and energy, so willing to forfeit any form of artistic practice for poorly paid contract work.

What would it mean to make self-permission a practice? To actually make a habit out of freedom — a collective freedom from internalized misogyny, self-hate, and doubt? Like all habits, it must be performed daily, even if only in the moments between work and sleep. A repeated gesture that eventually becomes instinctual.

Gripped with an urgency, I snapped my laptop shut and bolted down the library's stairs to the parking lot where I'd locked my bike. There was still some daylight left. I pedalled up Avenue du Parc toward the small mountain after which the city is named. There, on one of its low foothills, under the stone wings of Liberty herself, I spent the last of the day's light writing.

5

Allegorical Women

IF YOU VISIT MONTREAL, YOU'LL SEE HER — THE WINGED woman who guards the city. High up on a monument on the slopes of the city's centrepiece, Mont Royal, you'll catch our civic protectress in the act of stepping into the air. Nicknamed the Goddess of Liberty, the Athenian beauty extends her hand to the people. Below her stands the figure after which the monument is named: a copper statue of a middle-aged man in a dapper nineteenth-century suit, his hand also extended in greeting or blessing. This is Sir George-Étienne Cartier, one of the Fathers of Confederation. There are four women at Cartier's feet, two looking up at him, two gazing out at the city. At first glance, you might assume they're Cartier's relations or other historical figures, but then you notice they're all wearing Grecian robes and that their faces are identical, cast from the same mould. They represent New Brunswick, Nova Scotia, Quebec, and Ontario. At the rear of the monument are four other women, also with identical features and unseasonable robes, though with differing hairstyles. They represent the provinces that joined Confederation in later years. There are two more female statues, copper matriarchs with their life-sized children, nestled on the other sides of the monument. Could they be historical figures? Their clothes are more appropriate to the nineteenth century.

No, they're also allegorical figures representing Legislation, Education, and Strength.

When I was an undergraduate student in Montreal, I used to bike past the monument daily. Sometimes, after classes or work, I'd stretch out on one of its surrounding grassy slopes to read. I was happy to be living in a city with a female face — the face of a flying woman. She reminded me of Sophie Fevvers in Angela Carter's postmodern novel *Nights at the Circus*, a six-foot-two, curvaceous, peroxide-blond winged woman (half woman, half swan) who, after hatching out of an egg in a turn-of-the-nineteenth-century London brothel, goes on to join the circus and travel to St. Petersburg and across Siberia. These were all things I dreamed about doing myself — I, too, wanted to dye my hair, escape my egg, and travel across Eurasia by train.[1]

But Carter's precocious avian woman stands in strong contrast to Cartier's allegorical Goddess of Liberty. Whereas the Goddess of Liberty represents the concept of freedom, Carter's larger-than-life Sophie Fevvers embodies the possibility for women — real, historical women — to move beyond the allegorical figures that falsely represent them. As a novelist, Carter believed her task was to uproot the harmful myths about women's capabilities by creating a parody of those myths. To do so, she used a mix of what at the time were considered disreputable genres: gothic horror, science fiction, pornography, and fairy tale. "I am all for putting new wine in old bottles," Carter admitted in her essay "Notes from the Front Line,"[2] "especially if the pressure of the new wine makes the old bottles explode." Exploding myths and wine bottles, Carter aimed to form a new vocabulary for understanding women's power. When monstrous Sophie Fevvers first spreads her wings, she believes she'll herald a "New Age in which no women will be bound down to the ground." She quickly learns that this is much easier said than done.[3]

After reading Angela Carter underneath the Cartier statue, I began to look at Montreal's winged monument askance. The Goddess of Liberty was beautiful, solemn, and ahistorical. She was a copy of the winged victory that Carter's novel was parodying. Her serene Grecian face was a copy of a copy, fallen through time. She was accompanied by two lions with huge iron paws and mournful eyes. I ran my hand over one of their faces as I stared up at the Goddess of Liberty, thinking about Carter and Cartier, about fiction and history. About the promised age in which no women would be bound down to the ground.

As I gazed up at Cartier and his harem of provinces, I'd ask the question I'd ask again years later in the Elena Piscopia debate. Why was it that in most of the monuments I'd seen, the male statues represented historical figures and the female ones symbolized concepts? It's not that we lacked monuments of female figures, I realized; it's that we lacked monuments of historical women.

• • •

The first definition of *allegory* given by the *Oxford English Dictionary* is a "description of a subject under the guise of another subject of aptly suggestive resemblance." Yet there appears to be no aptly suggestive resemblance between the historical woman's lot and the concept she represents. Reflecting on the omnipresence of this phenomenon in her book *Monuments & Maidens*, the literary critic Marina Warner observes that justice isn't characterized as a woman in the City Hall in New York City or the Old Bailey in London because women were thought to be just. Nor were women considered capable of dispensing justice:

> Liberty is not represented as a woman from the colossus in New York to the ubiquitous Marianne, figure of the French Republic, because women were or are free. In the 19th century, when so many of these images were made and widely disseminated the opposite was conspicuously the case; indeed the French Republic was one of the last European countries to give its female citizens the vote. Often the recognition of a difference between the symbolic order, inhabited by ideal, allegorical figures, and the actual order, of judges, statesmen, soldiers, philosophers, inventors, depends on the unlikelihood of women practicing the concepts they represent.[4]

What Warner is saying is that the stark difference between the statues of female figures and the concepts they represent isn't just coincidental but deliberate. This is the central paradox for the women among allegorical monuments of women.

It almost seemed that if representing freedom and justice as female, patriarchy could, in a kind of sleight of hand, continue to deny actual women access to justice and freedom.

The more I thought about this paradox, the more I noticed it in different art forms. Justice isn't considered female because women were historically employed as judges, any more than the topless woman in Eugène Delacroix's depiction of the July Revolution of 1830 was an army recruit. If you've forgotten the title of the painting, as I did, just google "French Revolution Topless" and the image of *Liberty Leading the People* pops up.

I recalled Virginia Woolf's observation of the very similar contradiction between the female figures in literature and historical women: "Imaginatively she is of the highest importance; practically she is completely insignificant. She pervades poetry from cover to cover; she is all but absent from history."[5]

Because of this contradiction, allegorical women in bronze or in verse are much more than the allegories they represent. The allegorical woman is always already multiple. She represents both freedom and the unfree. As Angus Fletcher in *Allegory* puts it, "Allegories are far less often the dull systems that they are reputed to be than symbolic power struggles."[6] That was how I began to view the female statues I encountered in museums or in public squares — as power struggles.

Although created as containers for fixed meanings, the allegorical women crowding Cartier's feet are, in fact, imperfect vessels. They exist in the world as ahistorical symbols of virtue, and in the case of the provinces, symbols of stolen land. If they were perfect signifiers, why was I standing beneath the statue wondering what the Province of Saskatchewan had in common with this lady in a bedsheet? *Oh, what nice shoulders that symbolic power struggle has*, I thought, staring up at the impassive bronze goddess representing Education.

Standing beneath the Cartier monument, I wondered if there were any statue clusters in the city, or the country, or perhaps in the world, where the male figures represented concepts and the female figures historical women? I could find monuments of historical women and historical men, or of allegorical figures representing soldiers (*The Wounded Soldier* on Omaha Beach, France), nurses (Jeanne Mance tending a patient at the *Maisonneuve Monument* in Montreal), and immigrants (the *Angels Unawares* bronze sculpture in St. Peter's Square in the Vatican). I could find historical men and allegorical women, like the Cartier monument, but never allegorical men and historical women together.

Imagine a statue of women's rights activist Nellie Letitia McClung surrounded by three half-naked male virtues in togas representing Courage, Perseverance, and Wit. Certainly, McClung would have used the help of these virtues. They would have been especially useful when, in 1928, she battled with the Supreme Court of Canada over the rights of women to be considered persons.

In my search for monuments of historical women, I found a photograph of Nellie McClung online in Library and Archives Canada's collection. She has a broad, open face, warm but determined. A liveliness there, too, around the mouth, as if she was someone who laughed easily. Right thumb under her chin, left hand resting on a book. A thin gold watch snakes across her wrist. She looked strangely familiar to me, and then I realized she resembled my great-grandmother, Granny Morris, who left an impoverished home in Ireland where, forced into the unelected position of Angel in the House, she cooked and

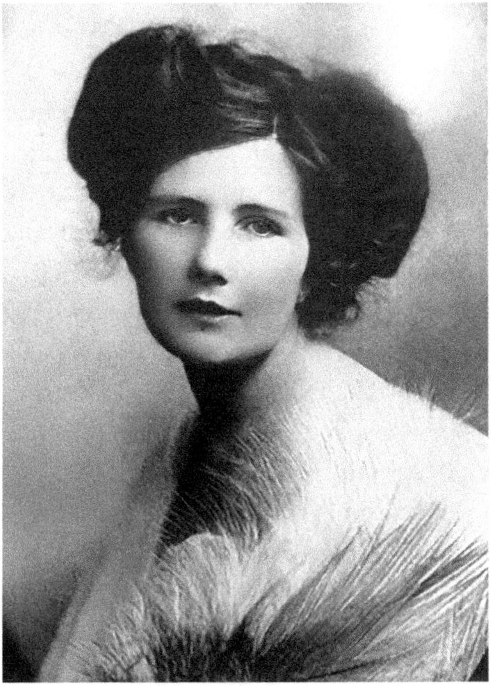

My great-grandmother, Kathleen Attracta Morris (née Lynch), as a young woman.

cleaned for her adult brothers. Rejecting this life, my great-grandmother sailed to England, trained as a nurse, and eventually travelled the world.

It's perhaps not surprising that there are so few monuments of historical women if up until this point women hadn't even been considered persons according to the British North America Act. This meant that women were therefore ineligible for appointment to the Senate. McClung and four other activists — Emily Murphy, Louise McKinney, Irene Parlby, and Henrietta Muir Edwards — took their case to the Judicial Committee of the Privy Council of Great Britain in London, then Canada's highest court of appeal. Their demand was modest by today's standards: that women be declared "persons" rather than property under the law.

In October 1929, Lord Sankey, Lord Chancellor of Great Britain, announced the decision: "The exclusion of women from all public offices is a relic of days more barbarous than ours. And to those who would ask why the word *person* should include females, the obvious answer is, why should it not?"

The law was repealed — a step toward emancipation, but only one for settler women. Indigenous women in Canada only received the right to vote in the 1960s, and on many levels, they still lack representation, rights, and meaningful acknowledgement of personhood. There's still a long way to go.

Near the Parliament Buildings in Ottawa, there's a monument to the "Famous Five" — Nellie McClung and her four fellow suffragists. It's one of the few monuments to historical women in Canada. Erected only in 2000, *Women Are Persons!* has iron-cast statues of the five women toasting their victory with a cup of tea. The artist, Barbara Paterson, chose to portray these Canadian political icons as ordinary women wearing plain period dresses, not Grecian robes, and to place them on the ground rather than on pedestals like other national political figures and monarchs. This was an effort to have the monument reflect the women and girls who might pass by it, who might pose for selfies with the women at the tea table or pause to read about their contribution to the personhood of women. Dispensing with the pedestal was a strategy to make history feel more accessible, to say, "This monument is for you."

• • •

There isn't much data to be found on the ratio of male-versus-female monuments, nor is there data on the ratio of monuments of allegorical women versus monuments of historical women in Canada. But in the United States there's something designed for just this purpose. University of Wisconsin–La Crosse art professor Sierra Rooney created the Monument Lab database to track the nature, prevalence, and economic backing of monuments in the United States from the "monument mania" of the mid to late nineteenth century to the early twentieth century. This was a time when Reconstruction and a desperate attempt to make sense of the horrors of the Civil War led to a degree of self-aggrandizement not seen before. During this intense period of monument building, statues of primarily elite, Anglo-Saxon men (and their horses) filled — and continue to crowd — the country's public squares. According to a 2023 study conducted by the Monument Lab, there are around three hundred statues honouring real women in the United States compared to about five thousand honouring real men in the country. That means only 6 percent of American monuments feature real women as their subjects.

Joan of Arc is the most represented woman in statues in the United States, Rooney's study shows, which is surprising because she wasn't American. In fact, America wasn't even a country when she existed, just a twinkle in the eye of the imperialist project. Perhaps Joan of Arc is so celebrated within the public square, and therefore public imagination, because though she's a historical woman, she comes closest to an allegory — a representation of bravery and defiance, of the power of faith. In this sense, the historical Joan has been eclipsed by her mythic persona.

As far as American-born representatives go, Harriet Tubman is the second-most honoured woman in the United

States, followed by Sacagawea, Rosa Parks, and Sojourner Truth. Yet at the time of the Monument Lab survey in 2023, there were twenty-two sculptures of mermaids versus the twenty-one honouring Harriet Tubman.

Why is the ratio of mermaid statues to statues of historical women important at all?

Monuments aren't history. As the Monument Lab points out, they're interpretations of history by people who determine who and what merit public honouring.[7] It comes back to the Padua debate about the inclusion of women in the square and Federica Arcoraci's point that spending time among all-male statues has "an impact on our lives and collective imagination."

To be clear, this isn't an argument for fewer mermaids — my favourite mythical creature since the age of five — it's an argument for more monuments of and for women.

• • •

The year I discovered Angela Carter, I visited New York City for the first time. I drove down from Montreal with a group of friends from high school. There were four of us, all in our early twenties, all from the same small town in the mountains of British Columbia. This was the first time we'd visited such a huge city, never mind such a famous one, whose streets seemed strangely familiar to us because of all the films and TV shows we'd consumed as adolescents. One friend grabbed my hand as we crossed the George Washington Bridge; she was staring out the window at the skyline in its smoggy pink haze, eyes glassy with emotion. Later, she confessed that as we went over the bridge she felt as if her body were swelling up with something she didn't understand — a homesickness for a place she'd never been to, a misplaced sense of pride for a city that didn't belong to her, a place that until this point she had no real interest in. She sensed she was witnessing something momentous, that her life was about to start. She also experienced an intense sense of discomfort.

I later learned the pathological term for this: *Stendhal syndrome*, a clinical phenomenon in which the presence of a beautiful piece of art or architecture or famous monument causes physical symptoms such as a racing heart, dizziness, abnormal sweating, chest pains, and loss of consciousness. The syndrome was observed by the Italian psychiatrist Graziella Magherini, based on one hundred and six cases of patients, all tourists, seen at the Santa Maria Nuova Hospital in Florence. These patients exhibited clinical symptoms that were consistent with the nineteenth-century French author Stendhal's writings after he visited the Basilica di Santa Croce in the same city. Almost two centuries ago now, Stendhal planned to visit the Santa Croce Chapel in Florence, which houses frescoes by Giotto di Bondone and paintings by Baldassare Franceschini, as well as the tombs of Niccolo Machiavelli, Galileo Galilei, and Michelangelo Buonarroti. As a monk opened the chapel gate, Stendhal knelt in awe. Of the experience, Stendhal later wrote: "I had reached that point of emotion that meets the heavenly sensations given by the Fine Arts and passionate feelings. Leaving Santa Croce, I had an irregular heartbeat, life was ebbing out of me, I walked with the fear of falling."

Dr. Magherini initially termed the condition *Florentine syndrome*, but it soon became clear that Florence wasn't the only city to induce dizziness and racing hearts. A similar phenomenon appeared to be afflicting tourists visiting monuments in other cities. In 1986, Japanese psychiatrist Hiroaki Ota coined the term *Paris syndrome* after observing several patients who, after visiting Paris, were suffering spells of dizziness, heart palpitations, shortness of breath and psychiatric symptoms ranging from hallucinations, both visual and auditory, to paranoid delusions and depersonalization disorders. According to Dr. Ota's findings, this monument sickness could have been caused by the major impact the traveller experiences when facing a significantly different culture and way of life than their own.

For four girls from a rural community in western Canada, New York City was Florence. But instead of a marker of the ancient world, New York with its noise and verticality was a gleaming monument to progress, money, and ambition. While we wandered, dazed, through Central Park, a man driving a horse and carriage yelled out at us, "Hey, Sex and the City, want a ride?" In that moment, we couldn't tell if we were strolling through a movie set or if this was real life.

We spent the day wandering among the city's museums and monuments. Not far from the New York Public Library, Gertrude Stein's bronze likeness sat Buddha-like in contemplation. We visited the Whitney Museum of American Art, which some years earlier, had hosted a retrospective of another monumental woman, the Cuban-American artist Ana Mendieta. In her *Silueta* series (1973–85), Mendieta created female silhouettes in nature — in mud, sand, and grass — with natural materials ranging from tree branches, moss, sand, fire, gunpowder, and on occasion, animal hearts. These *Siluetas*, which I only discovered years later, refused simple allegory. They redefined the nude, from artist's muse to a powerful and creaturely force of nature.

How different these *Siluetas* were from other monuments, how porous and vulnerable to their environment. In the artist's eyes, a dialogue between landscape and the female body.

In a 1981 artist statement, Mendieta said: "My art is the way I reestablish the bonds that unite me to the universe. It is a return to the maternal source. Through my earth/body sculptures, I become one with the earth."

But even a defiant and path-breaking artist like Ana Mendieta couldn't escape the misogynist traps of the art world.

In the early hours of September 8, 1985, Mendieta fell thirty-four floors from the Manhattan apartment she shared with Carl Andre, her artist husband. Neighbours had heard the couple fighting. In court, a doorman testified that he heard a woman screaming "No" several times around 5:30 a.m., and then the thud of her body as it hit the roof of the all-night delicatessen below. She hit the surface so hard that her head left an imprint.

In his 911 call, Carl Andre is quoted saying: "What happened was we had ... my wife is an artist and I am an artist and we had a quarrel about the fact that I was more, eh, exposed to the public than she was and she went to the bedroom and I went after her and she went out of the window."

Had she been pushed or thrown? Had it been an accident? Andre later claimed to remember nothing of the events leading up to her death.

Andre was arrested but subsequently acquitted of all charges. His lawyers used Mendieta's artwork — her themes of violence against women and her materials like blood and fire — to evoke a tortured artist and troubled person who would take her own life. But the portrayal of Mendieta as a tortured, suicidal artist didn't sit right with the people who knew her. They recalled the artist as passionate and ambitious with a voracious hunger for life. As a friend of Mendieta's recalls of their last conversation, only months before the artist's death: "She told me that she was making new work and that she was going to give up drinking and smoking because women artists did not get recognition until they were old. She said that she wanted to live long enough to savour it."[8]

• • •

Of all the monuments we visited on that trip to New York City, there's one I remember most clearly. Even in my memory, she rears up out of the water before me. After seeing her image replicated a million times on mugs, shirts, and key chains, cartooned and made miniature, I, too, felt my heart racing as I made my approach. *I walked with the fear of falling.* Standing on the ferry deck, my eyes pricked with tears. I understood why, when viewing her for the first time, the tourists lift their cameras. It's not to capture her image but to shield themselves from her gaze.

She's one of the only statues in the world you can enter and walk around in. You can climb up the 354 steps (twenty-two storeys) to her head, spend the afternoon there, and scratch your name along the inside of her skull. Through her crown, you might glimpse helicopters circling, passengers waving in delight at the puny human presence within the giantess's impassive face. She's the largest, most famous female figure on the planet; she's *Liberty Enlightening the World*. Visitors can possess the heart and mind of Liberty, but they must possess her at their own risk: People have actually died of heat exhaustion inside the statue in the summer months. The ordeal of the climb is part of the experience.

As visitors depart, looking up at the magnificent colossus from the deck of the boat ferrying them back to the city, they can delight in the knowledge that they've climbed under Liberty's skirts and moved around her interior landscape. A fantasy made real: The mightiest allegorical woman in recent history, she who possesses a scale that defies replication, is also so attainable, so easily penetrable by the common tourist. Part of the fantasy of entering the statue is due to the paradox of Liberty representing both the warrior virgin and the universal mother. Like Mother Mary, she can be both at once.

I didn't enter Liberty that day. I preferred to observe her from the boat where I could meet her austere gaze.

Although the statue's architect, Frédéric-Auguste Bartholdi, had originally asked his wife to pose for the monument's blueprints — which she did for the statue's gestation — it is, in fact, Bartholdi's mother's likeness we see in the overbearing, slightly grim countenance of Lady Liberty's face. Her face reminds me of the soldiers at the Soviet War Memorial in Berlin. The Statue of Liberty's physical and symbolic hollowness also means we can see what we want.[9] Liberty's torch can stand for Victory, or Fidelity, or Truth, just as the women below Cartier's monument could stand for Education, Grace, or Ontario. As the critic William Gass suggests, "The monumental monument tends to be … an open emblem. It tends to be FOR RENT."[10]

It turns out that the original Statue of Liberty was indeed for rent — symbolically but also in a more material way. Lady Liberty wasn't originally intended for New York City. A few years before construction, Bartholdi met with Isma'il Pasha, the khedive of Egypt, to discuss his plan for a giant sculpture inspired by the magnificent statues from ancient Egypt and the legends of the Colossus of Rhodes. It would stand at Port Said at the entrance of the Suez Canal and represent a woman standing on a pedestal wearing loose robes and holding a torch above her head. The work was to be given the colonial title *Egypt Carrying the Light to Asia.*

The proposal was turned down due to cost, but Bartholdi still clung to the hope of using his design. When the opportunity arose for an American-commissioned monument, Bartholdi did what all good artists and writers do and recycled elements from the failed Suez Canal project, refining the design to represent instead an American concept of liberty. On October 28, 1886, President Grover Cleveland led the dedication ceremony, claiming, "We will not forget that Liberty has here made her home."

In that year, when Lady Liberty made the United States her home (supposedly of her own volition), American women didn't have the right to vote and wouldn't have it nationally until 1920 — and then really only for some women. Due to voter-suppression tactics in many U.S. states, many Black, Latinx, Asian, and Indigenous women would continue to be denied voting rights until the passage of the Voting Rights Act of 1965. Lady Liberty made the United States her home at a time when African-American citizens suffered the harsh legacies of slavery. She became the symbol of a world power whose laws legalized sexual and racial discrimination. This giant female monument to freedom was a faulty signifier. She represented emancipation, but not women's emancipation. Liberty was not representing her own freedom.

It doesn't take much to see this contradiction now, but I can't say I noticed it when I first visited the monument. I was so accustomed to seeing female statues, and so acquainted with Lady Liberty's replications, including Montreal's own Goddess of Liberty or the Freedom Monuments of Riga, Latvia, and Kaunas, Lithuania, that I didn't question the phenomenon. Nowhere was Liberty representing her own freedom.

• • •

I still visit the George-Étienne Cartier Monument and sometimes in the summer I'll bring a book and lie under a tree, equidistant from the drum circle that forms at the monument's base and the LARPers (live-action role-players) on their allocated battleground. Every weekend they dress up in medieval regalia, and wielding artificial clubs and swords, fling themselves at one another. I realize I'm stationed between two epochs, a twenty-first-century drumming circle and a medieval war. Both groups follow a specific set of rules. I lie between them in my flattened grass mould like one of Ana Mendieta's *Siluetas*. If I close my eyes, history collapses, and their sounds blend to form the same scene. When I open my eyes again, I see the Goddess of Liberty with her beautiful, placid, Soviet face watching over the activities taking place below her.

Although these group practices follow long-standing rituals, they adjust and adapt. Several women have joined the circle with their drums — more now, I notice, than when I first started visiting the monument. The LARPers' weapons are made of foam. They use safe words. As I look out at the Cartier monument with its throng of voluptuous, toga-clad provinces and its winged protectress, at the centre, the tidy little figure of Cartier in his unchanging nineteenth-century suit, I'm reminded of Margherita Colonnello's words from not too long ago, arguing for a statue of a historical woman in Padua. Here, too, we need a very good statue of a woman in a very good place.

6

The Uncreative Life

You will find, as women have found through the ages, that changing the world requires a lot of free time.

— Alice Walker, *In Search of Our Mothers' Gardens*

1

TONI MORRISON'S IDEAL WRITING ROUTINE — A FANTASY routine because she never actually experienced it — is nine uninterrupted days in a room with huge tables. "I am reminded," Morrison mused in an interview, "of that tiny desk that Emily Dickinson wrote on and I chuckle when I think, Sweet thing, there she was. But that is all any of us have: just this small space and no matter what the filing system or how often you clear it out — life, documents, letters, requests, invitations, invoices just keep going back in."[1] Life — ordinary, imperfect, uncreative life — keeps interrupting.

This tiny writing desk is an island surrounded by a nagging sea of chores, or it's a life raft half capsized in the wash of living. Yet I still find myself seeking the perfect life raft or island. The perfect desk and perfect room, which, I imagine, would produce the perfect sentence.

• • •

Some years ago, a journalist I knew in Berlin conducted a series on artists' working spaces. Writers and artists were asked to send her an image of their writing desks, whatever that looked like, and she'd post them on her blog. Her request was clearly inspired by Virginia Woolf's thesis that in order to write fiction a woman needs financial security and a room of her own. The project wondered: How was this measuring up?

I sent the journalist a picture of my kitchen table, which I shared with two roommates at the time. It was small and square, painted blue, and flanked by a radiator and a hanging spider plant, the centre of our tight communal space. I didn't tell her that shopping lists were the only things I actually composed on this table.

At the time, I was renting a room intended to be a storage closet or a laundry room. It was large enough for a single bed, in my case a mattress on the floor, and the chipped, full-length mirror I'd found languishing on the street upon my arrival in the city. I'd also rolled in a clothing rack on which I hung the four dresses and single coat I'd brought with me from Canada. There was a window, tall and narrow, that let in a rectangle of light in the late afternoon. No room for a chair or a desk, hence the need to photograph the kitchen table.

One of my roommates was an actress who had, for the past few years, been struggling to find work. She complained, since she was aging — she'd just turned twenty-seven — that the struggle was only going to grow harder. When I moved into her flat, she'd just returned from Peru where she'd spent twelve days at a wellness retreat under the influence of a large amount of the plant-based psychedelic ayahuasca. In between excruciating stomach cramps and spontaneous defecation, she'd undergone a life-altering experience. She was lying helpless on the floor, vomit bucket beside her head, when she'd felt another presence in the room. Above her in the darkness hovered several tiny glowing lights. As they grew closer, they multiplied, but even amid all the discomfort, she understood that she wasn't in danger. These glimmering beings, my flatmate realized, bore a striking resemblance to the fairies in her childhood picture books, with their webbed wings and arched ballerina toes. They now loomed over her body, clutching tiny surgical instruments. Before she knew it, the fairies were operating on her. They sliced open her stomach with their miniature scalpels and began shifting organs around; upon finishing their business, they sutured the wound and disappeared through the ceiling.

When she awoke the next day, she felt an immense sense of well-being. For the first time in her life, she knew who she was. She'd also found her vocation. She'd leave her precarious acting career and become an alternative medicine practitioner.

My flatmate turned to me, blowing the smoke from her cigarette out the window in a distinctly German fashion. "And what about you?" she asked bluntly, pointing her chin in my direction. "You're a writer, but I never see you write."

She wasn't wrong.

Sometimes, between work shifts, which involved carting babies around the wealthy districts of the city or teaching English grammar to sullen art students at the Technische Kunsthochschule, I'd sit in a city park and fill a few pages of my notebook, but those sentences weren't leading to anything. They lay fragmented before me, imperfect.

Why did they have to be perfect?

"If nothing else is perfect," Bernadette Mayer once said, "why should a poem be perfect?"[2]

She was right. What use was perfection if it barred creation?

• • •

My roommate's observation — *I never see you write* — paralleled the questions the journalist was asking by requesting images of artists' workspaces for her blog. Is there such a thing as a perfect space for creation? If not bound by a dedicated desk, if not housed in a studio, does the creative life cease to exist? Does it just melt into the uncreative life, which is to say, into ordinariness?

To answer these questions, I turned, as I usually do, to books. In a small used bookstore in Berlin, I found a strange and beautiful 1970s novel by Laguna Pueblo writer Leslie Marmon Silko. I picked up *Ceremony* because I'd read Silko's short stories in an American literary anthology and had been haunted by her textual landscapes composed of drifting shadows and windy grasslands interfused, in reviewer N. Scott Momaday's words, with "a sharp sense of the way in which the profound and the mundane often run together."[3] A woman standing alone in a desert, her face turned away from the reader — this was the image I took away from Silko's atmospheric prose. But I knew nothing of the author herself.

In the preface of *Ceremony*, Silko describes the importance of space in allowing her to write her first novel. After moving with her young family from Arizona to Alaska in the early 1970s, she found herself sinking into a depression and in desperate need of a place to write. With her sons in daycare and in school, Silko explains, "I tried to write at home but I found it difficult to concentrate: the dirty dishes and dirty laundry seemed to cry out for attention."[4] Her creative drive was consumed by housekeeping. What she was seeking wasn't just a physical space but the mental space — away from tasks that somehow consume the mind, forcing the mundane over the creative — to write.

Luckily, a friend invited her to use the table and chair in his closet-sized law library in a building overlooking Ketchikan Creek. There, Silko had a view of the great Chief Johnson totem pole with Raven and Fog Woman, one of the most famous totem poles in the world, and a monument to women's power.[5] For the next six months, she worked on her Hermes portable typewriter until the legal services were moved to larger offices downtown. Silko, now an unofficial writer-in-residence to the law office, followed suit, but her new space had no door. Still, she noted, it was better than working at home.

Silko managed to get by in the room with no door for a couple of months until her friend informed her that he couldn't find a renter for the office space vacated by the legal services and that she could move back to the original office beside Ketchikan Creek. Delighted, she moved into the unrented space, now all her own. "Rent free," Silko writes, she was given "exclusive use of the space complete with heat and lights and, best of all, no telephone."[6]

But it wasn't just the space that afforded her the permission to write her first novel; it was a ritual as well. Silko notes of her process:

> My rule for myself was this: I had to stay in that room whether I wrote or not.... I'd walk over to the window to look up at the big black raven carved above me on the top of the pole. A long way down the pole came Raven's two raven helpers, Gitsanuk and Gitsaqeq, their raven beaks oddly hooked, melted from the fire's heat the time they carried Raven's gift of fire to human beings. Then came the figures of Raven and his wife, Fog Woman, who held two salmon by the tails. The beauty of the carved figures lifted my spirits and I'd finally break down my resistance, and start work on the novel.[7]

Being in this liminal space — a space that wasn't home and not the secretarial cubbyhole in the legal office downtown — opened up a new possibility for Silko: a space to dream, to commune with past storytellers and what she calls "old time stories" from different Indigenous Peoples. The title of the novel, *Ceremony*, refers to the healing ceremonies based on the ancient stories of the Diné and Pueblo people. It created the space for a writing ritual wherein the profound and the mundane could cohabit rather than compete.

Ceremony garnered Silko a MacArthur Fellowship (colloquially called the "Genius Grant"), which supported her through the years she spent working on her epic, *Almanac of the Dead* (1991). She acknowledged the effect of her cash prize (US$800,000 over five years) to *Time*, admitting she was now "a little less beholden to the everyday world."[8]

I appreciated Silko's comments on the material conditions behind writing her novel, those that temporarily released her from the responsibilities of the everyday. The work of genius I'd found in a used bookstore in Berlin hadn't sprung from the air but had been born out of ritual and strategy, a Hermes portable typewriter, and a view of Ketchikan Creek. And, something all writers wish they had, a generous friend at a law firm.

Toni Morrison notes a similar need for ritual to unlock her writing practice. When asked about her actual writing routine — not the imaginary one — Morrison talked about the importance for her to get up at the crack of dawn:

> I always get up and make a cup of coffee while it is still dark — it must be dark — and then I drink the coffee and watch the light come.... Writers all devise ways to approach that place where they expect to make the contact, where they become the conduit, or where they engage in this mysterious process. For me, light is the signal in the transition. It's not being in the light, it's being there before it arrives.[9]

One must create a ritual in order to make contact. To receive the "gift of fire."

• • •

With *Ceremony* under my arm, I hurried out of the bookstore to my nannying job. I recalled Morrison's dawn ritual, Woolf's utopian city of rooms, and the journalist's request for the evidence of a desk as I pushed my charge, baby Elio, around his affluent but still trendy neighbourhood of East Berlin. I thought of Elio's mother hiding in her office when I brought her sons back home, feeling guilty about claiming the space and time, but loathe to give up the room. As I navigated cobblestoned avenues with his industrial-sized stroller, I peered through people's windows into vast rooms of Scandinavian teak and white linen, spaces mostly unoccupied.

Fantasizing about spending afternoons in those rooms, free of any responsibility, I came up with a plan wherein the wealthy invite writers to occupy their rooms during the day. What was in it for them? They could become patrons of the arts at no real cost to themselves — perhaps only the expense of electricity to keep the lights on while the writer worked. Air Art-n-B. Who could I sell this idea to?

I considered telling Elio's mother about my plan, but perhaps she'd see it as a criticism of her relative financial security. Recently, she'd complained about her lack of productivity — that she'd spent the first hour of her precious study time writing and the next two deleting, word by word, everything she'd just set down.

• • •

For a long time, I'd been a habitual window-watcher, a voyeur into the indoor worlds of the leisure class. Most people watch reality TV to glimpse the interior lives and rooms of the super-wealthy, but I was more interested in the windows I could peer into at street level. Families swimming back and forth across their aquarium-like kitchens. A fellow au pair stooping to pick up a plate tossed onto the floor by a yellow-haired child in an artisanal high chair. A figure hunched over a phone absent-mindedly stroking the velvet ears of a sprawling Siamese cat. A woman tossing her hair in the recesses of a dining room.

In the evening when the lights came on, many of these rooms resembled the American artist Edward Hopper's paintings. He was one of my favourite painters at the time; his palette, like Gauguin's, was luminous with neon yellows and dark river greens. But I later learned that Hopper's genius, like Gauguin's or Picasso's, came at a cost to his wife, Josephine "Jo" Nivison Hopper.

Josephine Nivison was a successful artist when she met Edward. Her work had been shown alongside that of Amedeo Modigliani, Pablo Picasso, Maurice Prendergast, and Man Ray. At one time, *The New York Times* singled out her work for praise over that of Georgia O'Keeffe, her contemporary.[10] Yet Jo gave up her studio when she married Edward. As his career soared, hers dwindled. This was partly because Jo devoted herself to tending to her husband's career, handling the loan requests and other tasks of the uncreative life to clear the space and time for him to paint. She was also his only model: Hers is the figure in the lighted window, or the face in profile gazing out from the bedroom into the open city.[11]

"Of course," Jo writes in one of her diaries, "if there can be room for only one of us, it must undoubtedly be he. I can be glad and grateful for that."[12] That sentiment recalls Gertrude Stein's damning distinction between "geniuses" and the "wives of geniuses": a gendered divide that casts the roles of caretaker and artist as mutually exclusive. This was the case for the Hoppers, not because Jo wasn't talented but because the couple had determined there was "room for only one of us." It came back to the question of room. The private room or studio, yes, but also the room in a relationship, the sharing of space.

Something else I noticed: In the arcade of Hopper-like rooms I passed, there was a notable absence of books. It was an era of minimalism, of pale furniture and tall windows. Of dispelling anything that didn't spark joy. Sometimes the occupants of these rooms glanced up at me from their curated solitude and their expressions grew suspicious. They recognized a hunger in my face and grew startled, as if I were standing not outside, behind glass, but inside the room, sharing their air, their uncluttered, settled wealth.

They were wrong, though. I wasn't hungry for their lives as much as their rooms, the expanse of clean, liberatory space — though not actually private because I was looking in — in which, it seemed to me, one would be rescued from the uncreative life: One could do anything, be anything.

• • •

It wasn't just the rooms of the wealthy I was interested in. It was all kinds of buildings. When I first moved to Berlin, I spent every weekend exploring abandoned factories and hospitals. There were sanitoriums on the outskirts of the city that had fallen into ruin. There was a spy tower to the west. In a forest to the east, a large, deserted amusement park with a miniature village and a Ferris wheel that groaned in the wind. There were beautiful cloud-bleached buildings standing along the canal, long-ago factories waiting to be torn down.

I remember one building in particular — an abandoned sugar refinery not far from the city centre. NOTICE WHAT YOU NOTICE read the graffiti on one of the exterior walls. A group of us had climbed four storeys onto the roof. The stairs were still intact, but some of the floors had fallen away to join the open pit of rubble at the building's centre. We were now sitting in the sun, unzipping our jackets to cool off from the effort of the climb.

"Notice what you notice." At first the direction seemed redundant. Of course, you notice what you notice. But later that week, while I was standing in front of a class of German art students trying to instruct them in English grammar, the line returned to me. It was about the act of noticing. By tracking *how* we observe and not just *what* we observe, we learn more about who we are as observers, but also what kind of artists we could be.

What I'd noticed that day in the abandoned refinery was a mattress in one of the still-intact rooms, bare and pushed up against a wall. But the room itself was clean, not filled with dust and rubble like the other spaces in the building. Someone had been living there or was living there still.

There's a photograph of me in the sugar factory, one of the few from this period of my life. Someone must have taken it once we'd climbed down from the factory roof. I'm standing in a room in which three of the walls are missing. So is the roof.

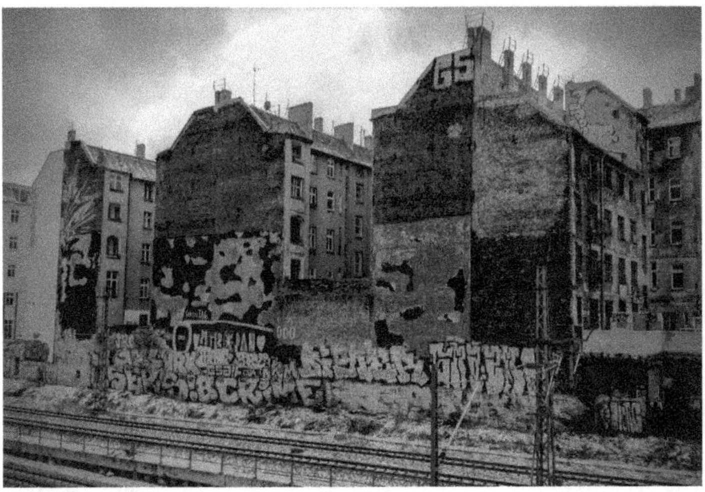

Abandoned buildings, Berlin.

All that remains is the square frame of the door and a part of the wall. Can this still be called a room?

Framing this room with a large rectangular window is another structure, also half demolished but nevertheless standing. I'm standing in a room within a room, a girl-woman, looking out of this window-door, out of the double ruins of history. I'm grinning hugely, on the brink of laughing, as if to say, *Look, I finally found a room of my own.*

2

Several years after the journalist's request, a poet asked me to write about my writing routine for a series he was doing on what a typical day looks like in a writer's life. I no longer lived in Berlin and was no longer carting toddlers around its annex. I'd given up that life and moved back to Canada to dedicate myself more formally to the study of literature. Still, despite taking on contract lectureships in order to support myself while trying to pursue this life, I realized I didn't have either of these: a typical day or a routine.

Although I'd been thinking about the importance of a workspace — a room with a key wherein the artist can sit around, as Gertrude Stein recommends, "doing nothing, really doing nothing," a nothing that inevitably becomes *something*— I realized, upon receiving his invitation that I wasn't practising what I preached. I'd taken on so many odd jobs to support my creative endeavours and had spent so many of my waking hours trying to hold the ordinary at bay that I suspected I might not know how to do anything else. I didn't have the room or the habit of freedom that Virginia Woolf specified. Or, it appeared, any good habits at all. I recalled science fiction writer Octavia E. Butler's advice to forget inspiration and rather form habits.

"Habit will sustain you whether you're inspired or not," she writes. "Habit is persistence in practice."[13] I needed to learn how to be more ritualistic with my time. To make a ceremony of time and space as Leslie Marmon Silko had done in her unrented law office above the creek.

The social theorist Henri Lefebvre saw the concept of everyday life — or what I'm calling the uncreative life — as a distinctively modern phenomenon, a product of capitalism, emerging in the nineteenth century as human existence and perception became increasingly industrialized and routinized. As workers congregated in big cities under modern conditions, the uniform and repetitive aspects of human lives gained visibility. But although my everyday revolved around repetitive work, my life felt provisional and sporadic, both industrialized and precarious, as I moved between teaching contracts and editing jobs. I was a child of the gig economy. Writing was something I squeezed between lesson preparation, laundry, and picking up my phone. It was something I did on train journeys between cities. Writing was something I did when unemployed and lying under a tree in August, or after reading a good book while inoculated into the sensuous atmosphere of another author's mind, thinking, *How can I stay in this place?*

I told the poet I'd map a day in the life for his series. To the best of my abilities, I'd try to be as accurate as possible. For the next twenty-four hours, I tracked the intersections between my ordinary, daily life and the one I thought I was living: the life of the mind.

I called it "Under Agatha Christie" because much of it was composed beneath Christie's poster in the mystery section of a nearby library.

• • •

I rise at 10:00 a.m. and make a path through the clothes on my floor — my floordrobe — to the bathroom. In the shower, I think of incredible things: the humpback whale I saw off the coast of South Africa, the red weather on Jupiter, a subterranean termite kingdom that runs the length of Brazil, a story told from the perspective of a woman who regrets nothing, not even her near-murder at the hands of her lover (it was the most attention he'd ever given her). I get out of the shower, stand in the hallway, dripping, and reach for my notebook, which immediately grows damp. For the next hour, I write, frantically, naked and cross-legged on my towel. When I return to these passages weeks later, I find that the text has dissolved into the paper. All that remains is an inky illustration of a whale's mouth, a hundred straight lines to indicate its baleen plate.

• • •

I climb two flights to the small glass room on my roof. In it, a school desk, a straight-backed chair with a velvet seat, and a teacup-sized cactus, nothing else. Here I sit and sharpen my tools. For the rest of the morning, I write about ordinary things: Portuguese custard tarts, the pair of miniature wool gloves found under a bar stool one night, a conversation with my sister in which she didn't ask me any questions except for "What time is it where you are?"

This glass room may seem invented, but it exists in a city I once visited. Since glimpsing this room, I've passed over its threshold several times (in fantasy, in dreams) to sit at its bare desk under its prismatic ceiling, like a spy in her tower, beaming messages to the world. Occasionally, I receive a signal that I'm on the right track. Follow this inquiry. This code. Suddenly, the whole city is vibrating. Even the cactus, the only unimagined object in the room, communicates with its tiny spikes.

Apart from this tower, spotted once from a window of my father's car, I don't have an ideal writing space. I wonder if this is perhaps my problem: To create this space you need both an empty room and an empty head. Right now, my head is filled with fantasies of a room on a roof that I'll never enter.

• • •

On my kitchen table lies an open book, two boiled eggs, and a slice of fruit. A military breakfast followed by a solemn procession to the library. I choose a floor with no children. For a moment, as I open my laptop, I'm convinced I live in a future that doesn't belong to me. No children, only skylights. Across the aisle, a serious woman, a librarian, murmurs into her rotary phone.

I sit in the section of the library dedicated to mystery novels beneath a poster of Agatha Christie surrounded by floating umbrellas. I'm beginning what promises to be a long and graceful sentence, a nimble, multi-clausal sentence, when my phone interrupts. Someone I haven't heard from in six months. Since the spring. "I need affection," he writes. Like that, the past vandalizes the future.

• • •

Agatha Christie wrote sixty-six detective novels, fourteen short story collections, and six novels under the pseudonym Mary Westmacott. She was a lifelong owner of dogs, with her preference leaning more toward terriers.

If I had a dog, I'd take her out for a walk before starting my daily writing practice. I'd watch her rush up to strangers, emphatically greeting them before turning abruptly and loping back to me. If I had a dog, she'd have a long, dark face. Her feet would disappear in the snow. She'd drift toward me like a gradual memory and then away from me, a ghost of something already forgotten.

I don't have a dog and so I have no excuse not to write. See how you've found me, alone at my desk, unexcused.

• • •

I'm standing before a class without my notes. They're somewhere in the floordrobe. One student raises a hand. "What is the space of innocence?" she asks.

"It's the space before anything has happened yet," I tell her. "The space that hasn't been corrupted by plot."

She frowns at me and then looks down at her lap where her phone lights up with important messages. I wish I could write as unapologetically and dexterously as this student who devotes herself, for the rest of the class, to typing quick responses into her phone.

I return to the lecture. A book hangs open in my hand, on the front page a photograph of a cactus. "Photography makes the particular universal," I explain to a silent room. Text is the opposite.

Is it? The sun is high in the sky. I've lost my train of thought. The roof of my imaginary glass room will be hot by now.

When I ask my students if they believe in love at first sight, they unanimously answer no.

• • •

Routine, from French for *route*. "Road, a way, a space for passage. Customary path of animals." From Latin *rupta* (*via*), "(a road) opened by force," cut through a forest, from *rumpere*, "to break."

I don't trust people who have written sixty-six novels. Like I don't trust people who claim they have no regrets.

• • •

It's not that I prefer sorting laundry, or invoices, or cleaning the bathroom drain to writing (though the former, I must admit, are satisfying); it's just that writing is the more terrifying of those tasks. It seems that when given the choice, like most people, I choose tedium over terror. Even though, as a notable horror film critic has argued, terror is the more progressive medium. Once I've pulled a sparrow's nest of dark blond hair from the drain, terror exchanges places with tedium. Now I'm ready to write.

But first I need to check the name of Agatha Christie's dog, to whom she dedicated her 1937 novel *Dumb Witness*.

• • •

Even Agatha Christie broke her routine, disappearing for ten days after learning of her husband's decision to leave her for his mistress. After finding her abandoned car, a Morris Cowley, parked above a chalk quarry, with an expired driver's licence and some of her clothes inside, thousands of police and volunteers raked the landscape in search of the author. A local lake was dredged, no body found. Her husband and his mistress were suspected of murder. Local newspapers published images of what the author might look like in disguise. On the tenth day of the search, Agatha Christie was discovered playing pool at a spa in the north of England where she claimed to be a tourist visiting from South Africa. She had registered herself in the hotel book under the last name of her husband's mistress.

• • •

Perhaps this is what it would take to finish my book: change my name and drop out of history for ten days. Or maybe there's more to be learned here. For a woman artist, taking time and space for creative work looks a lot like memory loss or an act of revenge.

• • •

I have no routine. I wish I did, because people with routines are happier, as are people with dogs. This has been empirically proven by scientists, whose profession it is to turn speculation

> into fact. It strikes me that this is the opposite task of the writer, who turns fact into speculation. And then there's yet another reversal in which fiction, due to its ability to capture collective experience, is mined for truth.
>
> I'm a scientist without a routine, without a dog, searching for abnormalities. This is what we, people of science and people of letters, have in common: an appreciation for things that have no histories, or that harbour hidden histories, things that don't fit.

• • •

As I tracked the day, I realized there wasn't such a strict boundary between these two, the creative and the uncreative life. Not only did they coexist, these two modes of living couldn't be separated.

And perhaps that wasn't a bad thing.

Perhaps they could even collaborate with each other.

3

There's a long history of everyday life — particularly the reproductive labour of maintaining daily life, like care work and housework — engulfing a female artist's time and attention. This uncompensated work has been the reason for the lack of women among monuments. Historically, while men were composing poetry, women were raising children. This predicament endures.

Alice Munro has often described the ways in which constant interruptions from relatives, children, and the looming household jobs necessitated her turn to the short form. "I did not 'choose' to write short stories," Munro writes in her introduction to *Selected Stories*:

> I hoped to write novels.... A child's illness, relatives coming to stay, a pileup of unavoidable household jobs, can swallow a work-in-progress as surely as a power failure used to destroy a piece of work in the computer.... I took to writing in frantic spurts, juggling my life around until I could get a story done, then catching up on other responsibilities.[14]

At the same time, Munro admits she can't imagine claiming a room — and even a desk — of her own. In an interview entitled "Writing's Something I Did Like the Ironing," she muses: "I can't tell you how horrified I feel when I go into a male writer's house and see the study, you know, the entire house set up for him to work. I just can't help thinking poor bugger. What a load to carry, it's really got to work, that novel, if everyone else is sacrificing for it."[15]

The novelist Gail Scott has also written about how interrupted time often shapes women's artistic output. "First, in terms of time, a woman's life is never simple," Scott argues. "She must put aside her time to do a million other things. Indeed, socialization has taught her to keep her mind so cluttered that it is often difficult for her to concentrate for whole days at a time in order to deal with a longer work like a novel."[16]

In *Silences* (1978), a study of the writing of women and working-class subjects, Tillie Olsen makes a similar observation to Scott's and Munro's, describing motherhood as being "instantly interruptible, responsive, responsible":[17]

> Children need one now ... the very fact that these are needs of love, not duty, that one feels them as one's self: that there is no one else to be responsible for these needs, gives them primacy. It is distraction, not meditation, that becomes habitual; interruption, not continuity; spasmodic, not constant, toil.[18]

In her treatise on Black life and creativity, *In Search of Our Mothers' Gardens*, Alice Walker writes of her own mother's working day, caring for the family and labouring beside her father in the fields, with "never a moment for her to sit down, undisturbed, to unravel her own private thoughts; never a time free from interruption — by work or the noisy inquiries of her many children." And yet, Walker notes, it was her mother who provided her with "the secret of what has fed that muzzled and often mutilated, but vibrant, creative spirit that the black woman has inherited, and that pops out in wild and unlikely places to this day." She likens her mother's care for her garden — the everyday gardening routines that bring about order and beauty — to the work of an artist. "Our mothers and grandmothers," Walker writes, have "handed on the creative spark, the seed of the flower they themselves never hoped to see: or like a sealed letter they could not plainly read."[19]

Feminized labour, reproductive labour — compulsory multitasking, interrupted time, and maternal guilt — shapes not only one's creative practice but one's thinking practice. Often it's simply a question of time that distinguishes the would-be artist from the working artist — the writer who composes lines in her head from the writer who puts words on a page. As Leslie Marmon Silko reminds us, writers need time and space free from the demands of the dirty dishes in the kitchen sink. Dropping out of one's life for ten days, fleeing to a hotel in Yorkshire, becoming a temporary art monster — that was one way to finish a writing project. But we aren't all Agatha Christie.

In the late 1950s, after a string of magazine rejections and being denied a Canada Council of the Arts grant in which she asked for money to hire babysitters, Alice Munro rented an office in Vancouver. It was to serve as a bare room where she could work uninterrupted by children or housework. "The solution to my life occurred to me one evening while I was ironing a shirt," reads the first sentence of the semi-autobiographical short story set in that office. "It was really the sound of the word 'office' that I liked, its sound of dignity and peace. And purposefulness and importance," the housewife/narrator of "The Office" confesses. Instead of dignity and peace, the writer is constantly interrupted by her attention-seeking office landlord who keeps bringing her gifts (such as a plant that requires daily care) to domesticate her bare office space, while simultaneously shaming her for acquiring a space in which to indulge her "hobbies" and neglect her family duties. The office isn't the room of one's own that she thought it would be. It becomes another place in which she must still play housewife. Eventually, the writer relinquishes the keys. "The Office" was the only story Munro produced during her months at the rented office. In the end, she had fewer distractions writing in her laundry room, which contrary to the image "laundry room" might bring up, was actually quite bright and warm.[20]

Maya Angelou had better luck than Munro in finding an office. In a 1983 interview with Claudia Tate, she describes her regular routine: "I keep a hotel room in which I do my work — a tiny, mean room with just a bed, and sometimes if I can find it, a face basin. I keep a dictionary, a Bible, a deck of cards and a bottle of sherry in the room. I try to get there around 7, and I work until 2 in the afternoon. It's lonely, and it's marvelous."[21]

• • •

Another reason there are so few women among monuments is that the "everyday" has often been depicted by philosophers as a quintessentially female domain, a country in which women are both citizens and prisoners. "Everyday life weighs heaviest on women," Henri Lefebvre once observed. "They are the subject of everyday life and its victims."[22] The idea is that while men have captained ships; chiselled Davids out of marble; built cities; invented bombs to destroy cities; held high office; and debated philosophies, such as the relationship between women and everyday life, women's lives have traditionally been contained within the realm of the quotidian, the insignificant, the indispensable yet unremarkable.

Simone de Beauvoir doubles down on this idea in *The Second Sex*, arguing that a lack of exposure to the outside world results in the foreclosure of true artistic genius. In a move similar to Virginia Woolf's conjuring of William Shakespeare's fictional sister, Judith, Beauvoir uses Vincent van Gogh's biography to comment on the narrowness of the lives of past generations of women:

> How could Van Gogh have been born a woman? A woman would not have been sent on a mission to the Belgian coal mines in

> Borinage, she would not have felt the misery of the miners as her own crime, she would not have sought a redemption; she would therefore have never painted Van Gogh's sunflowers. Not to mention that the mode of life of the painter — his solitude at Arles, his frequentation of cafes and brothels, all that nourished Van Gogh's art in nourishing his sensitivity — would have been forbidden her.[23]

Whether or not a brothel encourages sensitivity in its customers is up for debate, but Beauvoir's point is clear: a life hemmed in by the domestic limits artistic ability and opportunities.

• • •

I'm wary of the binary that pits the everyday against the life of the mind. I've always found Lefebvre's observation to be mildly insulting, because I'm often drawn to poetry, stories, images that arise from an engagement with the personal and the domestic. Historically, yes, most women have lived in the shadows of great monuments, trimming the weeds that grow about the statues of prodigious men. But even though they've been more tied to the rhythms of domestic work, that doesn't mean they haven't created art within the constraints of the quotidian. In fact, many women writers have spent much of their writing careers interrogating the everyday as a subject and a formal constraint — like the one you might use in a writing exercise. There's a creative resistance to be found in this practice.

Like the philosopher of the everyday, Michel de Certeau, I'd like to believe routines of daily life can be infused with acts of creativity. In his study of twentieth-century urban life, de Certeau argued that individuals navigate and negotiate power within the everyday practices of consumption, reading, commuting, and walking in the city — or, in my case, window-watching. Even the limited freedoms pedestrians have in shaping the city could be powerful. "The long poem of walking manipulates spatial organizations, no matter how panoptic they may be," he writes. "It creates shadows and ambiguities within them." In these shadows, beyond the censoring eye, flickers ingenuity and imagination.[24]

As a pedestrian, a window-watcher, I wasn't a victim of the everyday but a reformer. I chose my own path through the city, even if I was pushing a stroller and had to stop every few moments when baby Elio spotted a bird or a truck.

While Elio and I roamed around eastern Berlin, I recalled how Alice Munro propped a novel over the sink so she could read Fyodor Dostoevsky while doing the dishes. I thought of Emily Dickinson, who wrote in the pantry while skimming the milk. She wrote at her bedroom desk, the one Toni Morrison spoke of, the size of a hot plate, watching over her plants on nights when the temperature dropped below zero. This room she called "Freedom."

I imagine her now warming the plants with her hands, blowing on their leaves, penning in her looping, slanted scrawl: "The brain — is wider than the sky."

• • •

My Rilke moment — when I realized I "must change my life" — came to me a few weeks after my conversation with my flatmate about fairies. I was at a corporate fundraising event for an anti-corruption non-profit organization where I'd been hired as sole caretaker and entertainer for the guests' thirty children. Crouched in the grass behind the champagne tent, far from the stage, I painted butterflies and spiderwebs onto the kids' small, upturned, incorruptible faces. A young American woman, about my age, dressed in a tailored grey suit and silk blouse, gripping a binder to her chest, came up to me and asked if I knew where she could find a bathroom (she said "restroom"). The woman had a futuristic haircut, the sides shaven close to the contours of her skull, nails and lips painted the same liquid brown. She told me she was the keynote speaker and had to prep before her speech. I was almost mute with jealousy. What had I done with my life? The keynote's Americanness made her feel overly familiar in this European city. I felt I was looking into an uncanny mirror. But I showed her the bathroom.

I remembered the rule of perspective from my high school art class. *As objects get farther from the viewer, they appear to decrease in size at a constant rate.* I was disappearing. I didn't have the room of my own or the habit of freedom. I'd put myself through university, but even after I'd served as valedictorian of my graduating year, I was still drawing butterflies on children's faces. A little girl tugged my hand, reminding me I still needed to finish hers. She crinkled up her nose as I drew two antennae above her eyebrows and a little black-and-red hindwing across her right cheek. *Next Picasso.*

What had I done wrong? This wasn't the life I had envisioned for myself. I decided I needed to make a change, but what should that change look like? What conditions had to be met, not to be the Next Picasso but simply to live a creative life?

For the rest of the event, I sat in the sandpit and allowed the children to paint my face and pour sand in my hair. Across the lawn, someone was raising a flute of champagne to democracy. Eventually, as it grew dark, the guests came to collect their children, leading them away one by one to their suppers and bath times. Someone brought me a plate of food from the barbecue. I glimpsed the keynote speaker leaving with her colleagues, blazer now folded over an arm, directing her easy laughter into the night.

Over the next few years, I did change my life — that is, I managed to orient it more toward a life of creative and intellectual work. Now, a decade later, my life dedicated to the study and creation of literature, I find I'm still learning how to be more ritualistic with my time. To create a kind of ceremony of time and space within the everyday, as Leslie Marmon Silko did in her unrented law office above the creek. I realize that I may also have to accept that there's no escaping the mundane: I hold citizenship in both the creative and the uncreative life.

7

Everyday Monuments

A writer, I think, is someone who pays attention to the world.
— Susan Sontag, Frankfurt Book Fair, October 12, 2003[1]

Look closer, look again.
— Diane di Prima, Revolutionary Letter #36[2]

ONE ARTIST WHOSE PRACTICE AROSE FROM A COLLABORATION with the mundane is the American Language poet Bernadette Mayer. I didn't know much about Mayer until I began reading her poetry in the early months of the Covid-19 pandemic. Something about the extreme domesticity of this moment prompted me to seek out this poet whose particular care for the small and the ordinary demonstrates the value in attending to our everyday life. The value in looking closer.

A second-generation New York School poet — in college her poetry professor introduced her to the first generation, John Ashbery and Frank O'Hara — Mayer was a writer whose central project has been to create monuments to the unremarkable. Mayer was a genius of clutter, ephemerality, interruption. She managed to use domesticity not just as a subject but as a form.

Her youth was anything other than unremarkable. Born in Brooklyn in 1945 to a secretary mother and an electrician father, tragedy struck her family early on. "Everybody in my family died by the time I was sixteen," Mayer recalled in an interview. "My relatives were afraid that if they adopted me, they would die too. My father died of a hereditary condition at age forty-nine, so I thought I had to hurry up and do everything I wanted to do before age forty-nine."[3] Perhaps that's why she dedicated her life to finding creative possibility in every moment, to squeezing everything out of life that she could.

Orphaned and alone in New York, Mayer began writing poetry. She studied literature in the New School for Social Research, where she had her first encounter with the poetry of Gertrude Stein. When a professor observed that she sounded "a little too much like Gertrude Stein," she went on to read all the Stein she could get her hands on. She later admitted that Stein's poetry gave her a sense of permission, a sense of home: "I felt like *Oh my god, thank god someone has already written this, so I don't have to write it myself*.... Even in this stupid world there's a place I can exist."[4]

After graduating from the New School in 1967, Mayer co-edited the art magazine *0 to 9* where she worked closely with a wide array of artists and poets. Mayer taught writing workshops through The Poetry Project at St. Mark's Church in New York City, encouraging generations of poets to "work your ass off to change the language." Mayer was of the mind that we can't imagine what we can't describe; if the language of description is constraining, then the imagination can't be manifested into reality. Recall Simone de Beauvoir, who believed that women couldn't be geniuses. This constrained thinking was also a problem of language. To describe new pathways into existence, Mayer believed that was the poet's task.

It was this specific intersection of language and everyday life that Mayer was most drawn to describing. In 1971, for the month of July, the young poet set herself two tasks: to take a roll of film every day for the entire month, and to record six hours of corresponding narration to accompany the images. The goal: "to record all of the human mind that mine could see."[5] The work was mounted on the walls of a gallery and the words, read aloud and recorded, played out so that it would take the viewer a full day to hear and see the whole exhibition. "It's a diary of one month," Mayer explained. "I wrote incessant notes and made drawings about everything that happened every day. I wrote down as much as I could without interrupting my life.... I had chosen the month at random without knowing what I would be doing during that month, because I didn't want to choose a time to do this experiment that would be particularly loaded, or particularly interesting or dull."[6]

And that was what she did. *Memory*, her first major work, is a document of the everyday — its textures and shadows, its moments of boredom and intimacy. It was an attempt to document the present moment, "always there, to be entered, like the world of dreams or an ongoing TV show." To experience the whole exhibition, to see all the photographs and listen to the entire narration, was a day's work.

The narrated text accompanying the images has a clear Stein-like quality to it — sometimes swerving into heavy, relentless repetition bordering on abstraction:

> This is Kathleen this is kathleen here is kathleen here is kathleen kathleen is here she's doing the dishes why is kathleen doing the dishes why is she doing the dishes why the dishes why not the dishes kathleen doing the dishes she does them she did them last week she did them again she didnt do them right the first time why does she have to do them again do them again, she said. I'll do them again there she is doing the dishes again look at her doing them she does them typewriter teletape tickertape typewriter tickertape tele-tape kathleen is doing the dishes she's doing them again when will she finish when will she finish.[7]

The repetition — *here is kathleen, doing the dishes, when will she finish* — mirrors the cyclic nature of everyday domestic chores, what Rita Felski in *Doing Time* calls "the repetitive tasks of social reproduction."[8] Like Chantal Akerman's acclaimed experimental feminist film *Jeanne Dielman, 23, quai du Commerce, 1080 Bruxelles*, in which we watch Jeanne Dielman peeling potatoes for thirty minutes, *Memory* appears to slow time down. We, the listener/viewer, experience the monotonous nature of dishwashing in almost real time. We're also prompted to ask: Why is Kathleen always doing the dishes? Who has been producing this conveyer belt of dishes and why can't they help?

Who is saying she didn't do them right the first time? Perhaps Virginia Woolf's Angel in the House is hovering at her shoulder?

A typewriter merges with the sound of dishwashing toward the end of the vignette. Is this the poet Mayer's typewriter interrupting? Is it a daydream of a typewriter, indicating how Kathleen would rather be writing than washing dishes? Or is the poem suggesting there's something similar about typing and doing the dishes? That both are work and require time and perseverance? Is this convergence a means of bringing the creative and uncreative life together?

• • •

During a recent move, I discovered a box of notebooks dating back to 2020, the start of the global pandemic. That was a time of immobility, isolation, and overwork for me during which I experienced, in the words of the psychiatrist I met with, a major depressive episode. My uncreative life had overwhelmed my creative one. Although they depicted the same subject, the everyday, my diaries were nothing like Mayer's exquisite art piece.

I was living alone at this time, finishing a dissertation and a book, and teaching courses online in my contract job at the university. I rarely saw friends, since the law forbade us from visiting with anyone outside our immediate household. We occasionally met in parks, ate a meal at a picnic table, fending off the gulls, which seemed to grow more entitled as the pandemic wore on, flinging themselves through the air toward our fries. Then we each returned to our own apartments before the 8:00 p.m. curfew. On a few occasions, returning late from a park meeting, I jogged all the way home, arriving breathless at my front door as the city shut down for the night. If you didn't have a dog to walk, the fine for being out after 8:00 p.m. was between $1,000 and $6,000. This law led to some absurdist scenarios. For instance, in the early months of the pandemic, amid a surge in daily cases and deaths, police came across a woman and her husband out for a stroll in downtown Sherbrooke, Quebec, past the 8:00 p.m. curfew. The man was wearing a leash around his neck. When questioned by officers, the woman claimed she was walking her dog. The couple received $3,000 in fines.

I was lucky to have a job, affordable rent, distanced companionship, access to parks, yet I found myself paralyzed by the long, repetitive days holed up in my apartment. The world around me seemed to shrink, to be devoid of hope or oxygen. Lisa Robertson writes: "The biggest problem with melancholy is that it is more detailed than the world."[9] But my notebooks at the time weren't even filled with such details — that would have been more interesting. They were crammed instead with relentless attempts at routine, although the lists of daily tasks continuously overspilled the twenty-four hours meant to contain them.

One note reads:

> Memory
> Death
> Girlhood

Beside it is a restricted list of calories consumed and a schedule of minutes walked in a week. Another note reads: "Set up your life now live it."

It was exhausting to reread these notebooks. To see the same list of chores rear up again on each page, repetitive, unending, like identical tidal waves. It seemed as if there was no room for poetry amid the relentless administration. No room for wild thought, except occasionally in the margins of the pages. Looking back on these early pandemic notebooks, I realized why the tasks seemed insurmountable. There were simply not enough hours in the day or the week to complete the assignments I'd set for myself, and so each day had been designed for failure:

> 3 hours work on dissertation, 4 hours course prep & grading, 2.5 hours online teaching + office hours; milk and bread; answer emails. If time, call Dad. If time, go outside. Take down broken lights. Fluoxetine, 40 milligrams after 10 days. Move Ficus Andronicus closer to window. Grant deadline. Edit, resubmit. 77 calories in a boiled egg. As seasons change eyelashes thicken. Buy measuring spoons (green). Physicians graduate in June. Dissertation, even just 30 mins. Typo on page 5. Heimelich, belonging to the house, not strange; tame. No text without situation. Try doing the easy parts first.

The last directive was from my psychiatrist. It's advice I use for writing as well.

At the time, though, there didn't feel as if there were any easy parts. Everything seemed difficult, exhausting, and unglamorous. "Depression," writes Susan Sontag, "is melancholy minus its charms."[10] Or in Maggie Nelson's words, "Loneliness is solitude with a problem."

In a recent session, my psychiatrist had asked me about my professional goals. How did I see my life unfolding? she wanted to know. Finish my dissertation, I told her (at the time that felt like a Herculean task). Secure a postdoc, publish my book, find an academic job, even though I'd been told repeatedly that this was a near-impossible task in the current job market. I listed off my goals as the psychiatrist watched me through the small square on my laptop screen.

I found that I couldn't make eye contact with her, embarrassed and even apologetic for my ambitions. She was silent for a moment. When she spoke again, she suggested that my idea of success was too rigid.

"Try to be more flexible with the way you see your life," the psychiatrist said. "Your idea of what it means to lead a meaningful life."

"A meaningful life." The phrase was fitting as I was writing about the idea of the "good life" and its relationship to narrative, gender, and domesticity in my doctoral thesis. That night I dreamt that I met my psychiatrist at a house party. She was smaller in real life, or the real life of my dream. Not much older than me. She was gesturing with her hands. The music was loud, and I couldn't hear what she was saying.

Some months later, when I told a friend I was trying to be more flexible about my ambitions — trying to be less of a perfectionist in both writing and life — my friend frowned.

"I think it's okay to dream big," she said, "to want more. To be uncompromising about things." She thought I'd been given bad counsel.

Perhaps my friend was right. But I continued to think of what the psychiatrist had said, her advice to be more flexible about one's vision for life, for the shape of a life. This advice I added to my list of instructions in my notebook, along with the calorie counts and shopping lists.

Paging through the notebooks again, years later, I realized they contained more than just instructions and tasks. There was, I noticed, some rare moments when the deluge of orders dissolved and something nearing poetry washed fleetingly across the pages. The writer of these notebooks, past me, was still following orders, but they were of a different sort.

Over several pages, scrawled in a gloved hand — I infer this because of the jagged handwriting — was a description of my street, then another block, an alleyway. I recognized the glimmer of the all-night laundromat, three blocks south of my apartment, and the triangular park with the basketball hoop. This was Bernadette Mayer's Fourteen Blocks exercise. I'd found it online under her list of "Writing Experiments" — prompts she'd used when teaching at St. Mark's: "Structure a poem or prose writing according to city streets, miles, walks, drives. For example: Take a fourteen-block walk, writing one line per block to create a sonnet."

I'd followed this exercise several times. It was a reason to leave the apartment, but also a motivation to step outside the militant task list I'd set for myself, to reexperience the quotidian as a new sequence of images and sounds, rather than the repetitive march.

Other exercises on Mayer's list included reading a novel backward or purposefully trying to write a "bad poem." A liberating experience! Some exercises went further yet, verging on the impossible:

- Construct a poem as if the words were three-dimensional objects to be handled in space. Print them on large cards or bricks if necessary.

- Attempt to speak for a day only in questions; write only in questions.
- Write a work that attempts to include the names of all the physical contents of the terrestrial world that you know.[11]

There are experiments based on time constraints as well — to write in as much detail about a designated period of time. An experiment of that kind led Mayer to create her second major work, *Midwinter Day*, another great monument to the quotidian.

• • •

In 1978, almost a decade after *Memory*, Mayer tracked, through the medium of a long poem, a single day, December 22, the shortest or "least day" of the year. At this point, she'd left New York City and was living in Lenox, Massachusetts, with her partner and two young children. I picked up *Midwinter Day* again, a few years into the pandemic, as winter heaped its long, dark afternoons over me, as my daily routines began to feel even drearier, and the walls of my apartment a barricade rather than shelter. Every year, that season of dark domesticity felt like an accident. How did Mayer manage to make it beautiful? The dishes from last night's elaborate chicken dumpling soup lay scattered over the kitchen counter, the greasy cutting board shoved over the stove elements to make room for more dishes. But they could wait, I reminded myself, thinking of Jeanne Dielman at the kitchen table, of Kathleen at the kitchen sink, as I cracked the slim volume.

It was a small thing, to set aside time to read rather than deal with my chore list, but it was important. I was giving myself permission not to do the dishes. It wasn't yet midwinter, but the sun was low in the sky.

"This morning the axis of the earth began what the papers called its slow tilting return," Mayer wrote about December 22. "The sun will last one minute longer and the nights will be shorter. Lately when the sun sets it breaks through the hat of cloud on the sky like a person on the street who only glances at you, and then it begins to snow."[12]

As I paged through the opening sequences of *Midwinter Day*, the three-month-old kittens I was fostering settled at my feet, tracking my every movement with their feral-green, tarsier-like stares, reminding me, lest I should forget, that I was responsible for their feeding. I ignored them and kept reading *Midwinter Day.*

Like *Memory*, this long poem moves through the rhythms of the day's moments, from awakening to dusk, in Mayer's words, giving "a plain introduction to modes of love and reason" by proving "the day like the dream has everything in it." We follow the poet and her family to the post office, the shops, the kitchen, the cold driveway. We're suspended in bedtime storybooks, snowsuits, operatic tantrums, strip-malled landscapes, and in the "expensive sentences" that the poet writes in the dark hours when the children are sleeping and the house is temporarily quiet.

Midwinter Day, as the poet Alice Notley observes, "is an epic poem about routine," an epic about the repetitive and relentless tasks of social reproduction, tasks that traditionally fall to women: cooking, cleaning, childcare. But it's also about artistic routine: It's a test of the limits between creativity and dailiness, in which the poet cancels the distinction. For instance, as the speaker of *Midwinter Day* prepares a meal, the food begins to take the appearance of literary tools:

> [The] commas of the cheapest small onions for the sauce, the olive oil's drops on the map of the pot of tomatoes, letters of the straight pasta and the Poons in the soup with Twomblys, an arbitrary split moon of the half peas, the camera lenses of the lentils, homogenized script of the mass rice, foreplay with a nice knife at butter.[13]

Ingredients for a meal become the ingredients for a poem: commas, letters, scripts. They become landscape: map, Poons of trees, moon. They also become sensual: appetites for eating, loving, and writing stem from a similar need.

• • •

The pandemic sun descended below the trees in the park across from my apartment. Two skaters circled the informal ice rink produced by water buildup in the baseball diamond. Two gliding bodies looping into one on the ice.

I leaned against the window, trying to catch every detail. Mayer once observed that "each moment is a place you've never been." Meaning: each moment, however habitual, can be experienced anew. Ordinary moments can, in fact, be extraordinary, can be thick with possibility, if viewed through the right lens. It confirms to me the notion, in the poet Fanny Howe's words, "that seeing *what is* is a radical human gesture."[14]

Because of her ability to transform the ordinary into "a place you've never been," I didn't believe Bernadette Mayer saw herself as a victim of the quotidian. She might have seen herself as more of an archivist of the ephemeral. Her poetry tracks daily unremarkable moments in which, to quote a line that appears twice in her long poem, "Nothing Happens." But something does happen. That's perhaps Mayer's genius. In tracking what's considered "not art," she creates a tableau of daily survival. In bringing the questions of what it means to live a creative life and what it means to live a heavily domestic life into confluence, Mayer's work is, more specifically, about the daily survival of the female artist.

Tracking a day in which "nothing happens" is different from Gertrude Stein's assertion that to become a genius one must "sit around so much, doing nothing, really doing nothing." Doing nothing wasn't available to Mayer, who, at the time of writing *Midwinter Day*, was a mother of two young girls. It wasn't available to Toni Morrison, either, who was a single working mother of two, getting up at 4:00 a.m. each morning to write before her sons woke up. It was perhaps available to Leslie Marmon Silko, but only after she won a MacArthur Fellowship.

• • •

Mayer was writing and making art in an intellectual climate that too often pitted gender/identity concerns against experimental approaches. This includes the dominant feminist literary discourse at the time.[15] Experimental writing by women was seen as overly concerned with aesthetics and not politically useful to the second-wave feminist cause. Mayer's work pushes back against this discourse by foregrounding the interconnectedness of intellectual inquiry, artistic work, and domestic work. These are all spaces for experimentation. William Butler Yeats said that a finished poem should click shut like a box. But Mayer's poems stay open, porous. They invite the reader to collaborate. Even as I sat reading about midwinter on my couch, the apartment suspiciously quiet, I received their invitation.

A clatter from the kitchen, something wet and wooden crashing to the floor, pulled me away from Mayer's sentences. In the kitchen, the kittens blinked up at me, snouts smeared with chicken grease from the cutting board they'd managed to topple to the floor. I scatted them away from the crime scene and filled the sink with soapy water. *Here is kathleen, doing the dishes.* Kathleen was my grandmother's name. It was my great-grandmother's name. My name is a version of Kathleen.

When I returned to Mayer, the day was already half spent. But her poetry forgives interruption. It was produced through interruption.

• • •

Interruption is part of the reading experience. Part of our living experience. As Bernadette Mayer acknowledges: "If nothing else is perfect, why should a poem be perfect?" Why should a reading experience have to be perfect? Perfectionism is an issue of time and money. If there is no time or no resources to make something perfect, is that not also a fundamental part of the artistic expression?

Channelling Mayer's sentiment, American writer Amina Cain notes:

> I don't believe in perfection, and when it comes to fiction, it's a value I don't understand. Why should it matter? Is a short story, or a novel, or a work of art, or a film, meant to be perfect? Is it even possible? Do we write in order to create perfect things? I don't.[16]

Embrace imperfection, these writers suggest, as survival strategy. There was a kind of freedom to this — the permission to make imperfect work.

Mayer's line about perfectionism also reminded me of Jean Rhys, whose unfinished autobiography I was reading at the time. In the preface, her biographer and editor Diana Athill recounts a story of Rhys's deadly perfectionism. Five years after her magnum opus, *Wide Sargasso Sea*, was published, Rhys approached Athill, and out of the blue, admonished her editor for allowing the book to be published. "There is one thing I've always wanted to ask you," said Rhys. "Why did you publish that book?" When the indignant Athill asked what she meant, Rhys responded coldly: "It was not finished." Rhys then pointed out the existence in the book of two unnecessary words. One was *then*, the other *quite*.[17]

• • •

The imperfect survival of the artist. I'd been thinking about survival a lot during the long, dark pandemic years. How to balance the creative and uncreative life in a way that was energizing rather than depleting? What did that look like? What could that look like? Even now, as I write this, I don't have solid answers. I'm reminded of one of Mayer's writing instructions, though:

> Attempt to write a poem or series of poems
> that will change the world. Does everything
> written or dreamed of do this?[18]

In *Midwinter Day*, Mayer answers her own question:

> You think something like a book will change
> the world, don't you?
> I do, I take pleasure in taking the milk with
> the most cream.[19]

• • •

Shortly after Bernadette Mayer died in November 2022, a few of us went to visit a friend at a small farmhouse in upstate Vermont. The house was up an icy driveway on top of a hill called Blood Mountain. Our friend, a poet, had been staying there for two weeks, looking after the various animals that wandered around the farm: two large palomino horses; mother and daughter border collies, who both immediately thrust their noses into our gloves when we arrived; and two sinuous cats, a mother (thin, silver-grey) and her son (a sleek tabby), who blinked beside the wood stove like a pair of sphinxes. We'd driven down from Montreal along snowy highways. The road to Blood Mountain was frozen solid, like a vertical river winding up into the forest. I parked the rental car on the shoulder of the road, knowing it would never be able to get up the frozen cliff. We were rescued by another tenant of the farm, Austin, an artist from New York City who had originally come to the farm for an artist residency and had stayed. Now he ran a gallery in the nearby town and lived in a cottage perched on the hill just below the treeline. When he arrived, he instructed us to put on crampons before abandoning our car — I didn't and promptly fell face first on the ice — and then he kindly drove us up the hill in a pickup truck with chains. The border collies shadowed us up the road, herding us to our destination.

That evening, as we drank mulled wine around the wood stove with the cats sprawled across our knees and the dogs at our feet, I mentioned I'd been rereading Bernadette Mayer.

Austin immediately looked up. "Bernadette Mayer the poet?"

He told me he'd met her some years before. She'd been participating in an art-and-writing residency in the nearby town. "I didn't realize she'd passed away," he said.

"You *met* her?" I asked.

"I've never read her work."

"What was she like in person?"

I wanted every detail. This was the poet who had shown readers like me how to live with and within ordinariness and ordinary language, wildly and imperfectly. How to treat each moment, even the dullest ones, as a poem, a radical human gesture.

Austin thought about it for a moment, running a hand over the mother cat's grey coat. "Bernadette was very human, down to earth," he said. "She was punk."

8

Books We Sleep With

Now I was alone, except for books.
— Jean Rhys, *Smile Please: An Unfinished Autobiography*

DURING THE SUMMER MONTHS IN BERLIN, I OFTEN LAY DOWN after work in Tempelhof, the airport turned park in the south of the city, and lost myself in a book until the sun set. I had the feeling of being swallowed by the book. After a few hours, I emerged disoriented like Jonah from the belly of the whale, hair smelling of brine. Recently, as I bemoaned the fact that in all those years in Berlin I'd produced nothing of substance, a former roommate reminded me of my reading habit. "You complain of not writing," she said, "but I never once saw you without a book."

It was true. Reading and note-taking can be a kind of artistic practice. As the author Angela Carter writes, "Reading a book is like re-writing it for yourself.... You bring to a novel, anything you read, all your experience of the world. You bring your history and you read it in your own terms."[1]

Although I didn't publish much during those years, all my notebooks of that time are scribbled through with lines and ideas prompted by the books I was reading. Sometimes the notes were about the act of reading itself. One of the books I was reading was *The Private Lives of Trees*, a short novel by the Chilean writer Alejandro Zambra. I wrote down his dictum on reading: "It would be better to close the book, close the books, and to face, all at once, not life, which is very big, but the fragile armor of the present."[2]

Was reading, I wondered, a way of avoiding the present? Or was it rather a way of suspending the present in order to be fully contained in a bubble of time? For when you're reading, you're in a state of suspension. Hours pass with no airplanes overhead. Grass grows wet with dew. Contrary to being a passive experience, reading is an active practice. Each sentence is a unit of movement. When reading, you're in the act of arriving.

After a time, I decided to formalize my practice of reading by applying to graduate school — to become, as we used to joke, a professional reader. For this, it seemed to me, was the first, most important task of a writer: to read everything.

But, as I'd realize, this would come at a cost.

• • •

When I finally left Berlin, I exchanged a human being — brown-eyed, alert, filled with complex nerve endings and a fluency in several languages — for a stack of books the length and weight of a person, a stack that now occupied the left side of my bed. For some years afterward, I regretted the trade — or rather, I wondered if the trade had been necessary. Maybe it would have been better, as Zambra writes, to "close the book, close the books" and face life in all its largeness and fragility through a different lens. And yes, as the Russian literary theorist Viktor Shklovsky reminds us, "to live in any real way is painful." But in the end, I had to accept my decision. I'd followed Rilke's advice however difficult it was to do that at the time. I'd changed my life.

If you asked him, my former love, he'd say I exchanged him for a city, a program in which one is required to read a book a day and not a slim book, a fat one with tiny margins and no dialogue. Although it's true I left Berlin to pursue graduate studies, the exchange wasn't so simple. In the end, I left a more domestically oriented life for one shaped by the abundance that books offer us but also by the solitude they bind us to.

The pursuit of an intellectual life and the desire for intimacy shouldn't have to be mutually exclusive. Yet, I find for many women — particularly women writers, academics, and artists — this continues to be the case. They're faced with a choice between the cultivation of love, companionship, and family, and a retreat into solitude and creative work. Of this gendered double standard, the poet and essayist Leslie Adrienne Miller writes: "The image of the male poet in retreat can be attractive to society. But the image of a female poet in retreat is somehow against nature, a liability that can lead to emotional bankruptcy."[3] There is, then, a form of solitude that attends the female artist, one that suggests deviance, stubbornness, abnormality, and precarity. As we've seen, this goes all the way back to the Renaissance belief that women were physiologically indisposed to being intellectual, casting female genius as monstrous.

• • •

After first reading about Mary Cassatt in Jamaica Kincaid's *Lucy*, I decided to look up the nineteenth-century artist's paintings online. Like Gertrude Stein, the independently wealthy Mary Cassatt lived and painted in Paris most of her life. She befriended the impressionist Edgar Degas, supported the suffragette movement, and never married. "Women," she once wrote, "should be someone and not something."[4]

Scrolling through her work, I was struck by how many paintings there are of women reading. Many of them are modelled on Cassatt's older sister, Lydia, to whom the painter was devoted. An 1878 painting, *Lydia Reading the Morning Paper* (a.k.a. *Woman Reading*), depicts a woman with reddish-blond hair, relaxing on an overstuffed green armchair, absorbed in a newspaper. Her right hand is casually poised to turn the page. We see Lydia again, this time seated on a wicker bench in the morning sunlight reading a paper, framed by roses, and again, lounging in a silver armchair, immersed in her book.[5] In another work, *The Pensive Reader*, drawn with pastels, ochre, and blue, a book lies open on the table as the reader, in sustained concentration, leans over its pages, resting the side of her face on her palm. How often have I read like that?

While a woman reading as a subject might seem fairly benign, in the context of the late nineteenth century's debates about women's education, these images of women reading — and especially reading newspapers about current affairs — carried with them a whiff of revolution. In some quarters, a woman's claim to a reading life and to a public life was discomforting and even threatening.

Around the time Cassatt was painting her portraits of women reading, an education law was passed in France — the controversial Camille Sée Law of 1880 — authorizing for the first time the establishment of secondary schools for girls. This seemed like progress for women's rights. However, though the Camille Sée Law did offer girls secondary education, it also carefully defined a course of study for female pupils that wouldn't prepare them for the baccalaureate examination and would consequently bar them from higher education and access to the professions.[6] Two steps forward, one step back.

As I gazed at the portrait of Mary Cassatt's pensive reader, it occurred to me there's still something covertly subversive about women reading — a particular solitude or separateness unique to the female reader that disrupts and disquiets.

• • •

In late 1789, Mary Wollstonecraft — philosopher, women's rights advocate, and mother of Mary Shelley, author of *Frankenstein* — put together an anthology for women entitled *The Female Reader*. This was to be the first anthology or textbook compiled by a woman, though the cover doesn't bear her name. As her husband, William Godwin, explained, Wollstonecraft in her literary career "conceived a vehement aversion to being regarded by her ordinary acquaintance, in the character of an author, and employed some precautions to prevent its occurrence." In other words, Wollstonecraft didn't always give herself permission to claim the title of author. Godwin added more cryptically that although Wollstonecraft was the sole author of *The Female Reader*, the book "from a cause not worth mentioning, has hitherto been printed with a different name [Mr. Cresswick] on the title page."[7]

The Female Reader was designed as a pragmatic guide to enable women to function as intellectual adults. For Wollstonecraft and the other proto-feminists of the eighteenth and nineteenth centuries, reading was a technology of access, a way of introducing women, though not including them necessarily, to a worldly conversation. It promised a retreat from domestic obligations and an entrance into public life. Despite some contradictions in its argument, the anthology constituted one of the time's most advanced articulations of a woman's right to think and to be educated and contained the embryo of what would be one of the earliest works of feminist philosophy, *A Vindication of the Rights of Woman.*

Learning to read, and learning to read critically, Wollstonecraft believed, was the path to women's emancipation; it was the only way to level the playing field for the real-life versions of Virginia Woolf's fictional Judith Shakespeare. "Strengthen the female mind by enlarging it," Wollstonecraft wrote, "and there will be an end to blind obedience."[8] Although many of her arguments for women's rights were ridiculed by her peers — one conservative aristocrat responding with a satirical piece claiming that if women should have civic rights, why not plants and animals, too — Wollstonecraft continued to strive for women's education throughout her short life. She fought for what she considered the "new genus": professional women authors compensated for their writing.[9] She knew it would be a long journey requiring centuries of women's activism, but that didn't deter her. She encouraged the generations of activists that followed her: "The beginning is always today."

We see the same gesture two hundred years after Wollstonecraft's *The Female Reader* in Elena Ferrante's globally renowned Neapolitan series. One reason Ferrante's novels are so popular is that they foreground reading as a radical act, one in which we, readers, can participate, revealing the ways in which the female reader is a threat to the patriarchal order. As a precocious and brilliant child, Lila issues library cards in all her family members' names to access a world beyond the grey courtyards of her neighbourhood, though even this doesn't allow her and our narrator, Lena, to shape a life that isn't patrolled by arrogant, dismissive, and abusive men. Of their voracious appetite for knowledge, Lena observes of her herself and her friend, "She was trying to understand, we were both trying to understand, and understanding was something that we loved to do."[10]

Reading, *understanding*, for these writers relays a direct access to power. The female reader is a powerful reader. But at the same time, she's a neglectful woman. Was this really still the case today? What is the role of the female reader in our era? What is at stake for women when we open a book, when we turn our critical attention away from the demands of our everyday lives and toward the open conversation of the page?

• • •

"I read, much of the night, and go south in the winter." In university, a professor drew our attention to that line from early on in T.S. Eliot's *The Waste Land*. He read the poem as an expression of sexual stagnation and emotional barrenness. In this section of the poem, the speaker, Marie, is reading, he said, so that means she isn't having sex. The line has stayed with me ever since.

She is reading, so she is not conceiving children.

She is reading, so she is not listening to you.

She is reading, so she is alone.

Or she isn't alone but separate. She's in what Friedrich Nietzsche calls "the inward cave, the labyrinth of the heart" into which "no tyranny can force its way."[11] She's reading and so is locked within a solitude of her own making and her own protection.

"To write, to do any kind of work well," notes Amina Cain in her study of the writing life, "we must at least have a solitude of mind, a solitude of seeing." This solitude of mind, this solitude of sight, can be accessed in such moments of retreat. As Cain writes, "We retreat to read. We retreat to think."[12]

"I read, much of the night, and go south in the winter."

To me, this sounded like pure heaven.

• • •

As I thought about T.S. Eliot's Marie reading at night, about Lydia Cassatt reading the morning paper, it occurred to me that one reason the solitude of the female reader might be more political, more controversial, than that of the male reader, is that time operates differently for women — or so we're made to understand. Women's bodies, we learn, are living clocks that can't keep pace with men due to their biological utility. As men careen to the peaks of their careers, many women find they are faced with a paralyzing set of questions and decisions to make about their bodies, procreation, timing. Lydia Davis, whose writing has been described as a "grammar of loneliness," sums it up well in her one-line story "A Double Negative," in which a female narrator contemplates whether to have a child. At a point in her life, she realizes that it's less about wanting a child and more about not wanting *not* to have a child — not wanting to feel she's missed out.

It was stressful to exist in this double negative, this knot of nots. This was another reason to turn toward books, to live in suspended time, to find refuge from the impasse that this double negative evokes.

• • •

Someone I went on a date with during this time told me that at thirty-three he was the prime dateable age for a man. The prime age for a single woman was, of course, significantly younger. I'm not sure why he told me this — it certainly didn't earn him a second date. Perhaps it was to remind me that the cards were stacked in his favour, that men age more productively, increasing in value with each grey hair. As proof, he cited charts exhibiting the "official" decrease of women's desirability and the increase of men's desirability. I looked them up later. Like two mountain peaks, one red, one blue, they change course over a person's lifespan. The red (female) peak experiences a quick drop off after the age of twenty-three, while the blue enjoys a long, luxurious decline down the slope of desirability. Similar charts depict deeply entrenched racial biases, too.[13] These charts make painfully legible the systemic racism and sexism that shape not only our desirability but our desires.

As the man I went on a date with spoke, I sensed that I'd suddenly become a stranger, not to him but to myself. I often felt this with men. A kind of estrangement from myself. Of course, this man's rant wasn't new to me. As Susan Sontag wryly observed, women "are old as soon as they are no longer very young."

A no longer very young woman sitting across from a boring man in the late afternoon — I'd seen this vision in many a coffee shop window. Now it was my turn. A line drifted into my head at that moment: *Our bodies are never entirely useful and never entirely beautiful.* And then I wondered, where had I read that? Or did that thought belong to me?

Whether or not the thought was mine, the lesson was clear: What I'd learned over my girlhood and young adulthood, what I was trying to unlearn, was that for women, love, durable intimacy, and companionship were part of an economy of scarcity. This is how it has historically been construed and continues to be presented by social media. Apparently, with each year, women's stock depreciates. As British writer Olivia Laing reflects in her study of loneliness, *The Lonely City*, single women in their mid-thirties find themselves at an age where "female aloneness is no longer socially sanctioned and carries with it a persistent whiff of strangeness, deviance and failure."[14] This "whiff" of strangeness haunts the female reader as she claims her separateness from the world, when she bows her head to the page rather than the baby monitor.

• • •

"There's never a right time to start a family," a doctor once told me unprompted during a routine checkup. "I just wouldn't want you to regret it later."

"Do you have children?" I asked her. I'd just turned thirty.

"Yes," she said proudly. "I have four."

Regret. The word took on a particularly gendered connotation in this instance. I thought of the Lydia Davis short story, and a knot of anxiety rushed to my chest. I didn't want to carry with me that "whiff" of abnormality, failure, and prickly eccentricity — did I? Not having a child, it seemed, was the worst possible case of FOMO a woman could experience in her lifetime. Despite my resistance to societal pressures, I could feel myself being pulled in.

Years later, though, the anxiety lessened. This was thanks to the conversations I had with other artists in my community, women, queer, and nonbinary friends, conversations about the books we were reading, about our projects, about our strategies for navigating a world that's still largely hostile rather than enabling to many of us. The desirability charts and metrics of our youth-obsessed culture dropped away — there were so many better uses of my time and attention. I recalled Alice Walker's words: "A writer, to be connected to the world, should have a circle that cares about the world. And out of that would come the writing." I focused my energies on building this circle.

• • •

I won't describe my past life here, because if I did, I'd have to describe my former love. I'd have to tell you about how, as we prepared for sleep, he'd turn to me and say, "Last look," before he switched off the light, so that we could memorize each other's faces in the moment before the blackout. This was so that we'd recognize each other if by chance we should share the same dream.

I no longer meet him in my dreams. Or if I do, we no longer recognize each other. In the words of Pablo Neruda, "the same mouth / is now another mouth." We pass each other without a second glance.

For some years, I instead found myself dreaming about strangers — often celebrities or acquaintances and their children. There was one particularly well-photographed family that I became obsessed with for a while. I'd known the couple in the early days of their courtship. Their lives seemed to move seamlessly from one rung to the next of the vertical ladder of success — engagement, law school, marriage, baby one and two, CrossFit, bucket list, *Live, Laugh, Wine.* Miami vacation, two-bedroom home in the city traded for five bedrooms in the suburbs, renovations, dark cabinets to white, reclaimed wood and half-marathons, gymnastics tournament. Public declaration of ongoing spousal commitment on a vista in Aspen, Colorado.

Without knowing it, I'd memorized their kids' tiny faces in all the configurations of joy and despair captured by their many daily, hourly, updates. Theirs were the last faces I saw before going to sleep. They were my "last look." Along with acquaintances from university crouching in front of Machu Picchu, ads promoting a new miracle diet (ice cubes and self-discipline), kitten videos, pug videos, a heavily documented Christmas vacation in the Galápagos Islands, brunch, group brunch, someone's glamorous selfie with a toilet in the background. These were the last images to be imprinted on my retina, the visions I'd bring with me to sleep.

For this reason, I started sleeping without my phone. Banished, hypnotic, it pulsed in the far corner of my room. But I wouldn't be seduced. I'd resist its lure with the self-determination of the ice-cube dieter. Although sometimes I'd wake up in the middle of the night and stalk across the room to check it. For a time, I made a rule: Only books were allowed near my bed.

• • •

During this period of my life, I frequently met up with friends who were also thinking about female solitude and its relationship to reading. We agreed that solitude didn't necessarily mean loneliness. To be in solitude wasn't to be against community or against love. One could enter into solitude with others. Find a version of aloneness that, to borrow Susan Sontag's words, was "nourishing — not just a waiting."[15]

I made an open call for friends to send me photographs of the books on their nightstands, the books they were currently "sleeping with." Their photos make up the following collage.

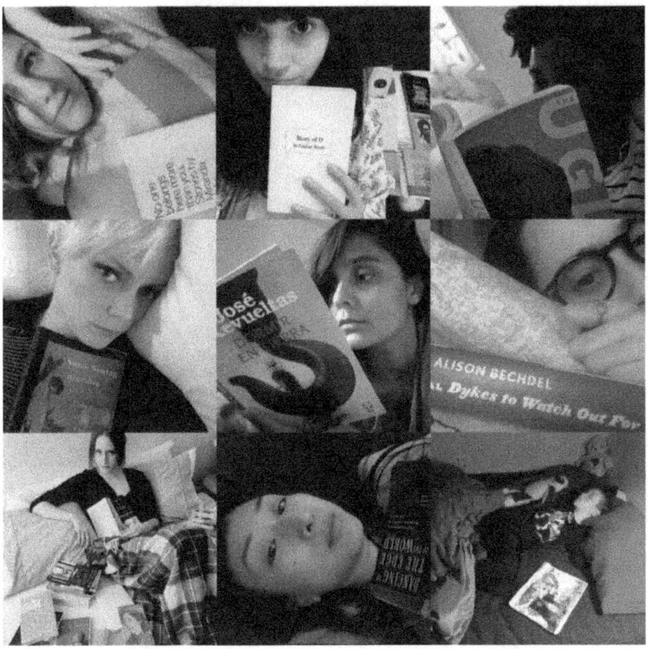

Books we sleep with.

• • •

How to take down the patriarchy? Build a network of brilliant and difficult women. Sleep with more books.

Forming a "Solitude Collective," some of us started making meals together, reading books by women and nonbinary writers, meeting every few weeks at a different member's home. Everyone in this unofficial collective/reading group came from different backgrounds and experiences with solitude, loneliness, and intimacy. One member of the group was surfacing after the breakdown of a long-term relationship; another complained of a series of disappointing intimacies, or the prevailing insistence on informal relationships; some craved nonconventional modes of companionship. However, due to circumstance, or choice, or a refusal to settle, many of us realized we'd been categorized as difficult women. Misfits. Killjoys. There was something about female solitude that frightened or aggravated people.

"I feel as though couples think I'm scrutinizing them or judging them," said one member of our reading group. We'd been discussing American short story writer Lucia Berlin's *A Manual for Cleaning Women* that evening, and some of the members had started to pack up to go home. I was sitting beside her on the couch under a large monstera plant that cast a bat-like shadow on the wall behind her.

"It's been a hard winter," she said, pulling her legs beneath her on the couch. She said she'd been alone for much of it. For the most part, she enjoyed her life, but sometimes there were these holes of loneliness, of indecision. Weekends could be especially tough.

There was a passage in one of the Berlin stories we'd read that night that had particularly resonated with her. A line about the "long hollow feeling of Sundays. No mail and faraway lawn mowers, the hopelessness."[16]

"I know exactly that feeling," she said. Those hollow Sundays filled with difficult feelings. The *hopelessness*. And here she laughed. Was it contagious? She worried that people thought it might be and would avoid her.

I considered what she'd said about difficult feelings. The cultural studies theorists Sara Ahmed and Sianne Ngai have argued that dysphoric feelings make legible the inner workings of a broken system: They're not simply a problem to be fixed but rather a response to structural injustice.[17]

I said something like that to her. At least I mentioned Sara Ahmed and also Ann Cvetkovich, whose book *Depression: A Public Feeling*, I'd been reading at the time. Part memoir, part medical history, Cvetkovich's book reflects on why intellectuals, activists, and those seeking space for creative thinking so often struggle with feelings of hopelessness and self-loathing.[18]

Disappointment, dissatisfaction, irritation, these are political emotions, I told my friend. They're useful and dangerous. Or, rather, they're useful because they're dangerous. They signal that something is wrong on a larger social scale.

"What if I don't feel like being political," she said. "What if I just want to meet someone?"

That wasn't the response I was hoping for, but it was a valid one, too.

Later, on my commute home, I recalled a line from one of my favourite books — Anne Carson's *Autobiography of Red*. It tells a story of unreturned love, a familiar story, though the beloved is the Greek hero Herakles, and the unrequited lover is a small red monster named Geryon. When Herakles eventually discards Geryon, he declares, "I want you to be free."

And poor Geryon responds, "Don't want to be free want to be with you."[19]

That exchange has always stayed with me. Freedom can be lonely.

• • •

It wasn't lost on me that solace and solitude share the same root: *sol* from the Latin, meaning "sun." I found myself orbiting these two heliotropic words/worlds. I slept among dead authors but living books. I slept beside living authors and silent books that lay, opened, awake, beside me. In a way, this experience wasn't dissimilar to sleeping beside a lover. There was the alien consciousness encased in the soft shell of the book. There was the quiet, angular weight, the blunt spine, the pages warm and musty as skin. "What makes lovemaking and reading resemble each other most," the writer Italo Calvino observes, "is that within both of them times and spaces open, different from measurable time and space."[20] The reader submits to the act of reading. She forgets herself, suspended, as Lisa Robertson puts it, "in the vertigo of another's language."[21] To be shaped by a text, by the contact with another's innermost thoughts — this is a form of pleasure.

It is a form of love as well.

For, as the cultural theorist Lauren Berlant observes, "what being in love secures is the evidence that you have had an impact in the world by being a condition of possibility for someone else."[22] To be a condition of possibility for someone else isn't only to be someone's fantasy but to be the conduit for that fantasy. This isn't unlike the relationship between the reader and the book.

To love then is to read. To be loved is to be read.

• • •

Even after this transitional time in my life, books have remained my cure to the overstimulation of the screen and the small but cumulative disappointments that seem to crowd the seams of each day; they have become the soft technology that mediates the hard, flickering machinery of my waking life. More than simply a retreat from life, they offer an entry point into understanding life. They are the trapdoors into what Virginia Woolf in her diaries referred to as "the real world," the expansive and private world of the mind.

Now, years later, when I have a moment to myself, usually in the bathtub or in a hotel room when I'm travelling alone, I lean into the lamplight, and enter into a slow communion with my book. I enter into a space beyond measurable time, the space of the page, where, in a matter of hours, a whole life can be changed.

9

This Is My World

If we opened people up, we'd find landscapes.
— Agnès Varda, *The Beaches of Agnès*

1

TO REACH MY CHILDHOOD VILLAGE, YOU HAVE TO DRIVE through a mountain. I remember trying to hold my breath during the long tunnel ride that separated the coast from the semi-desert of the Little Karoo. I believed that if I didn't hold my breath, the mountain might collapse on our car, smothering my mother and brother and sister. I was responsible for holding it up.

Our village was in a valley surrounded by the low hills of the Riviersonderend, a range of sandstone peaks named after a literal translation of the Khoikhoi word "Kannakamkanna," River-Without-End. This small town — with its white Dutch Reformed church and old communion houses, its apricot orchards, dusty roads, and mud-red irrigation dam — has become synonymous with my childhood.

It's never winter in my childhood, and this must be because of the desert light, the broad yellow days that govern that part of the world. I can still remember the prick of fear upon hearing the hyenas' manic falsetto and the wild shrieks and barks of baboons from the caves in the hills. After immigrating, we never returned to South Africa as a family because we didn't have the resources. But my siblings and I often talked about our village and our old friends, comparing memories. The pale clay roads; Violet, the little white firewood pony who sometimes pastured in our backyard when released from her duties of delivering wood to the town; the malt chocolate Popsicles we bought for fifty cents at the village's only store; our friend's mom who read us Grimms' fairy tales without omitting the violent parts; the Santa Claus Parade in the middle of summer; Auntie Dott, who smoked in bed, whose duvet cover was cratered with burn marks from the cigarette ash, and who died one night in a house fire — these stories we described to one another in a game of Remember When. I was always startled by how much my brother and sister remembered; they were only nine when we moved.

"Remember when the boomslang crawled into the laundry basket?" asked my sister. "And you almost walked on it when you went to the toilet at night? Remember when Mom called the neighbours and they put towels under the bedroom doors so it wouldn't get us?"

"How could you remember that?" I asked her. "You were sleeping — and you were also six years old!"

"Remember when we stole apricots from the neighbour's orchard?" my brother chimed in. "And he set his geese on us?"

"I don't think he set the geese on us. They were behind a fence."

"But they chased us — I remember running. He had vicious geese."

"Remember when J and C came to visit for Easter and the tree in our garden grew chocolate branches?"

"Remember when we went camping in the bat cave?"

"Remember the Owl House?" This last question was mine.

"We never went to the Owl House," my brother said.

"No, but we heard stories about it. Do you remember the one about the woman who lived there? The artist?"

We heard about the Owl House, not from the 1984 Athol Fugard play, *The Road to Mecca*, or the film of the same name, but from a family friend, J, who spent time there. Once, on her way back to Cape Town, she brought us a sculpture of an owl with huge eyes made of dark glass. It was arrestingly beautiful. And a little frightening, the way those eyes sank into the face like pools of black water. But children are often attracted to things that are a little frightening.

My siblings said they remembered J well. We loved when she came to visit. She was tall, very witty and warm, drawing us up into great bear hugs. She lived in Cape Town and taught art at a college, so when she visited she brought art supplies and treats from the city.

In the 1970s, J frequently visited Helen Martins, the reclusive artist who lived in the Owl House. J and Helen became close friends, J being one of the only people Helen let into her life. But when J spoke of her friend, which she did rarely, there was a sadness in her voice that I recognized even as a child. On the day that she brought us the owl sculpture, I remember thinking that I wanted to know more about this otherworldly creature and the woman who had created him. When I think back on that memory now, I wonder if it was the idea of the independent and unconventional woman artist that most attracted me — that a woman could dedicate her life to art at the exclusion of everything else. That this was a possible path for a girl.

• • •

Helen Martins was born in 1897, ten years after one of my favourite artists, Georgia O'Keeffe. Martins was born in the opposite hemisphere, though, and in a remote village in the Great Karoo. Nieu Bethesda, "Place of Flowing Water," was named after its secret water source, vital to the farming community in the area. In fact, Nieu Bethesda was so remote that it was the last village in South Africa to get electricity, in the early 1990s. Before that, the villagers relied on candlelight and paraffin lanterns, whose smell I still remember from my own childhood (our home didn't have electricity till the late 1980s). As a young child, I distinctly remember my mother turning down the gasoline and the flame disappearing into its blue centre.

Martins also resembled Georgia O'Keeffe physically. She was a slight woman, intelligent and curious, with a striking, dark-eyed beauty. Like Jean Rhys, another daughter of the colonies born around this time in Dominica, Helen was named after a sister who died, as if she was a replacement for the lost daughter. Helen trained as a teacher in the nearby town of Graaff-Reinet where she met and married a fellow teacher, a dramaturge. The two travelled around the country, putting on amateur theatre productions for small audiences, but the marriage soon fell apart. The dramaturge was unfaithful and controlling, by all accounts a boorish man. There were rumours that he coerced Helen into having two abortions during their six-year marriage. After several attempts, Helen finally left her husband. At the age of thirty she returned to her family home in Nieu Bethesda to look after her ailing parents, and there she remained for the rest of her life. That was also when she began turning her home into an art piece. After her parents died, she stayed in Nieu Bethesda, isolated, solitary, absorbed in her work.

It occurs to me now that Helen Martins was a kind of art monster, though not the sort Jenny Offill discusses in her example of the genius Vladimir Nabokov and his caretaker wife. Martins was an artist who was deemed monstrous by her community *because* she was both a woman and an artist. She was named a pariah because she lived in her house alone, without a man, because she turned her kitchen into a studio, because she lived her art, just as she lived inside her art.

But is it possible to live comfortably inside one's art — for art to provide complete shelter? It seemed that Helen Martins was testing this.

2

I returned to South Africa for the first time in my early twenties. I was pursuing an M.A. at the University of Toronto at the time and had applied for a three-month scholarship to do research for a writing project on outsider figures in rural communities. I immediately thought of Helen Martins, the mysterious artist fossilized in the amber of my childhood. Martins was a classic outsider artist — defined as an artist whose work is "created from solitude" in an "exalted feverishness" with little contact with the conventions of the art world.[1] I was determined to find a way to her house.

I visited my old village and some of the people we'd known when we lived there. But upon arrival, I discovered I could no longer speak Afrikaans, a language I'd once been fluent in. Sitting across the table from a dear family friend, someone I'd often chatted with as a child, the words caught in my mouth. It was a strange feeling — to know someone so well but no longer be able to communicate with them. In the attic of our old home, which was still owned by my uncle, I found relics of our former life: photographs, letters, even some old toys. There were tape recordings of birthday parties and community plays and one from 1994 of President Nelson Mandela's inaugural address. All were covered in more than a decade's worth of dust.

Among the photographs, I found several of my mother's old friends, including J, on one of her many visits from the city. In one photo, we are all squeezed together on an outdoor couch, wearing hand-knitted sweaters and holding up sparklers. The game was to write your name in the air before the sparkler ran out. I was struck again by what a loving community of friends we had during my childhood in South Africa — a large, social, nurturing chosen family, a family of women — and how alien the idea of the insulated and private nuclear family felt when we moved away from this community. I remembered J's stories about the Owl House. I'd looked up the Owl House's website, so I knew it existed, but I still wondered if this mythic place I'd heard about throughout my childhood could actually be located on the map.

The village I grew up in sits on the doorstep of the area known as the Little Karoo. I knew that the Owl House was east, in the Great Karoo — more than seven hours away by car. But I had no car and, more importantly, no driver's licence.

This was a major problem and seriously limited my ability to move freely. Everyone seemed to drive here. Well-off families owned multiple vehicles. In rural areas, those who couldn't afford cars walked along the side of the roads, hoping for an open-back truck, a *bakkie*, to pick them up and ferry them a few kilometres in the right direction. There was little public transportation. Sometimes they walked for hours.

I was able to secure a lift from the Western Cape to Graaff-Reinet, the closest town to Nieu Bethesda. There I overnighted in an old Cape Dutch house belonging to an elderly lady, a distant family friend. When she learned that I wanted to visit the Owl House, she warned me that there was no way to Nieu Bethesda without a vehicle. It was a good hour away, at the end of the road. No buses went there.

I found a taxi stand beside a large Victorian building, the post office, in the centre of Graaff-Reinet. Several off-duty drivers, smoking in the post office's shade, glanced up at me as I approached. I greeted them in English and asked how much they would charge to drive to Nieu Bethesda and back. The men frowned at me. One of the drivers, a younger man, said something and shook his head. I was in the *Groot Karoo*. No one spoke English here.

It had been twelve years since I'd spoken Afrikaans. Even then, it had never been my first language. I'd learned it by listening and so it had always felt improvisational to me, unfettered by grammar rules as English was, though of course I knew that books and plays had been written in this language. It had rules; I just couldn't remember them. There was something about leaving the verb until the end of the sentence. I tried to make my request again, this time only using words I could remember. Please. *Asseblief.* How far. *Hoe ver.* How much. *Hoeveel.* And I said the name of Helen Martins's village again, a lisping biblical word that seemed to exist between languages. *Nieu Bethesda.*

To my surprise, the young man was able to decipher my garbled request and answered me, carefully repeating his words when noticing my uncomprehending stare. This time his words, opaque at first, turned over in my brain, revealing a sudden glimmer of meaning. I understood that his name was Simon. He'd pick me up first thing in the morning. Bring cash. There was no ATM where we were going.

• • •

The road to Nieu Bethesda is lined with giant willows. They appear suddenly on the side of the road, momentarily enveloping the dry world in their looseness. Other visitors have noted their presence as well, their startling incongruency in the semi-desert landscape, a hallucinatory green amid the orange dust.

As we dipped into the valley's basin, I spotted the tiny white steeple of a Dutch Protestant church, the telltale sign of a colonial settlement, a village in the folds of the valley. How similar it was to my own childhood village, tucked into the folds of the valley. Then the Victorian houses came into view, verandaed and gabled, sun-faded red and green corrugated roofs, each with small, shuttered windows. All the walls were plaster washed in white to deflect the sun, though it was winter now and the sun was welcome. I recalled touching the walls of our neighbour's house when I was a child, my hand coming away chalk-white.

We reached the Owl House just as it was opening for the day. It was a modest home with a sloping corrugated iron roof over the veranda, the stairs heading to the porch, framed with cactus trees. It seemed to be looking inward, its handsome stained-glass windows impervious to the visitor. I offered to buy Simon an entrance ticket, but he declined. He'd meet me back outside in an hour.

• • •

I spent my childhood in the desert, so I know why the Karoo house is built to be so dark, the windows diminutive and shuttered, the clay floors a polished sheet of ice in winter, cool as a cave floor in summer. Here houses are stone wells, but instead of storing water, they preserve precious cool air that, along with the sparse shade of the willow trees, determines the economy for survival in forty- or fifty-plus Celsius weather. But to live your whole life in such darkness, to rarely leave the enclosure, would be stifling.

A reclusive woman alone in her house in the desert, employing local farm labourers to assist her in her artwork, Helen Martins struck an odd figure. Some believed her to be a witch. Others thought she was conducting an affair with one of her art assistants, thereby crossing class and colour lines in apartheid South Africa: a scandal. It's no wonder Martins kept to herself, hardly venturing out into the street and communicating only with a few friends and her assistants, Koos Malgas and, before him, Jonas Adams and Piet van der Merwe, whom she employed to help her create her art. In this hostile environment, she went about bringing the world to her home, slowly transforming her house and its fenced-in backyard into her protected domain.

Once Helen Martins inherited the house from her parents, her first task was to let the light in. She moved sections of the walls and replaced them with cathedral-coloured glass. I noticed the colour immediately as I entered the house: the strange red light flooding the kitchen, the modest bedroom, an undersea casement with heart-shaped mirrors, awash with a radiant emerald green. The light filled the house like a mood, like a human presence; I felt as if I were walking through an exquisite, obsessive, even slightly terrifying mind. Crimson mirrors, dark wine bottles, framed illustrations from a biblical textbook. The coloured light sparkled on the walls and ceiling as water on the roof of a cave. Running my hand over the wall, I realized it was studded with crushed glass. Martins had ground the glass in her coffee maker and used it to decorate the walls and ceiling of her home. In the kitchen were rows of Mason jars filled not with lentils, beans, and rice, as I first thought, but crushed green and red and pearl-coloured glass. There's a story about how she went about decorating her house with crushed glass. One image that stays with me is Martins standing in the centre of the kitchen beside Adams, throwing the ground glass up at the freshly painted ceiling, delighted as the air shimmered around them. Adams closed his eyes to the falling glass dust, but Martins kept hers open. She was unwilling perhaps to give up one moment of beauty, one moment of astonishment, even if it could harm her. She wanted to witness every part of the art process.

I wandered through the glittering rooms, enthralled by their eerie domestic tableaus. A print of the *Mona Lisa* on one wall, a depiction of the three wise men on their camels that was very similar to the illustrated Bible that I remember reading as a child. In one of the windows, a leaping deer whose hindlegs seem to dissolve, sea horse–like, into a piscatorial tail. Framed portraits of saints and Victorian children, Dutch biscuit tins, and carved into the wall, a huge fish with a blue glass eye. In the room known as the Long Bedroom stood three narrow beds with lacy pillows and threadbare covers, lined up beside each other as if waiting for Goldilocks to test them.

• • •

The inspiration for Martins's sculptures came from a mix of canonical art, kitsch, and ordinary household objects: the lions on the matchbox, the graphic on a medicine bottle. One story goes that when Martins first met Malgas, her long-time assistant and collaborator, she provided him with cement and an empty sardine tin and asked him to make a relief of the picture of her Anadin headache tablets label, which was an image of a 1950s housewife holding her hand to her brow. The migraine lady in the sardine tin still rests on a window ledge at the Owl House. Delighted with Malgas's reproduction, Martins hired him on the spot in 1964. Malgas stayed on at the Owl House until Martins's death. He went on to create a larger version of the migraine lady on the water tank.

I was captivated by the wash of colour, the strange undersea light that permeated each room, yet at the same time, I felt I was pressing against a submarine weight — the loneliness of being a woman and an artist in a small, close-minded village. Despite its beauty, I sensed this was a space of nightmare as well. In one room slumped a small round figure in a baby's cap, its squinting, pockmarked face like a gnawed apple. Two small legs protruded from its sack-like body. When I got closer, I noticed one foot ended in a shoe; the other, in a hoof. This sinister creature, who could well have emerged from Hieronymus Bosch's Hellscape, is named *Little Devil.*

• • •

The Owl House contained its own mythology. It reminded me of Angela Carter's subverted fairy tales and allegorical parodies, and her celebration of kitsch and low-brow artforms. I wondered if Helen Martins was engaged in a similar project to Carter's: siphoning new wine into old bottles so the pressure of the new wine makes the old bottles explode. Certainly, Martins made use of old wine bottles, transforming them into coloured glass windows or decorative skirts for her life-size statues. She also delighted in combining low- and high-brow artforms: *Mona Lisa* alongside the migraine lady in the sardine can. But it's hard to know if these amalgamations were created with irony or if they were simply a celebration of the world's tired and wondrous images, its cultural driftwood washed up on the desert shores of Nieu Bethesda.

Martins wasn't formally trained as an artist. Glasswork and sculpture were crafts she took up, quietly and in relative isolation, once she returned to Nieu Bethesda after her divorce. I wondered what drove her to reinvent her parents' house and turn a space of domesticity into both an artist's studio and an art practice. The website for the museum that now maintains Martins's Owl House cites boredom as her impetus for making art: "Driven to despair by the dullness of her daily life, she took steps to transform her world with light, colour and texture." I couldn't imagine boredom being cited as the sole catalyst for a male artist or even for other more well-known female artists, like Georgia O'Keeffe or Leonora Carrington.

Other accounts mention rumours of an oppressive and predatory father. Trauma, these reports suppose, was the reason for her move to artmaking. Although these reports remain unconfirmed, Helen's father lived the last several years of his life in a room outside the house, whose walls Helen painted completely black. Inscribed in the concrete steps leading up to its door was the designation THE LION'S DEN. The room's windows had been bricked up as well.[2] Had she confined her father to this black cell to punish him for his crimes?

The notion that her genius was born solely of boredom or of trauma seems dismissive to her talent. For the work that awaited me outside the back door to the house was born of a phenomenal vision. It was clear to me that Helen Martins had always been an artist, but it was only when she was granted the space and the independence — without a domineering husband or father to impede her — that she was able to realize her practice.

What I remember, as I stepped out into the yard, is a distinct feeling of relief at being outside again, back in the Karoo winter sun. I had been uneasy in the house, I realized. I could sense Martins's claustrophobia and isolation there. As I opened the back door, I caught my breath at the astonishing sight that greeted me: mermaids in pools of clear water; winged camels with the hooked beaks of birds; wise men, hands lifted in prayer; kneeling prophets; children, long-limbed and ecstatic, frozen mid-leap among pyramids; Eve clutching the forbidden fruit, a snake winding about her waist; gleaming peacocks with feathers of crushed green glass; giraffes' heads sprouting from the ground and human-sized cats; owls with giant glass eyes like the one I'd seen when I was young; sun worshippers with their arms thrown up; cement replications of the monoliths of Easter Island; a miniature replica of the town church with a painted clock on its steeple (Martins prayed here on Sundays instead of at the actual village church); women in wine-bottle skirts, women resembling angels, all of them with their hands raised as they crowd together facing east — or what Martins believed was east — toward Mecca. Above the procession a wire sign nested into the fence: THIS IS MY WORLD.

This garden was Martins's interior landscape, reflecting her spirit even more so than the rooms in her house. Here, in the Camel Yard, there was the joy of making art, of seeing a world take shape, of gathering a community, even if its members were cast from concrete. The joy of creating a meeting place out of glass, concrete, and metal scraps.

Surrounded by these ecstatic stone people and animals, I didn't feel alone. In fact, I felt as though I were taking part in a parade or a rally — the Christmas parade in my old village where Santa rode through the streets in a donkey cart loaded with gifts or the peace march I attended as a teenager, protesting the invasion of Iraq, or even the dizzying feeling of standing in Times Square with my girlhood friends some years earlier on our first trip to the monumental city. Martins had brought the world to her garden.

• • •

Later that morning, in the museum shop where I bought a few postcards and a replica of one of the glass-eyed owls, I read of the circumstances of Helen Martins's death. Now I understood J's sadness, her reticence to speak of her friend who had created the Owl House and the Camel Yard. After so many years of working with crushed glass without protective eye gear, Martins began to go blind. "I cannot keep my eyes open not for anything," Martins wrote to a close friend. "Should the doctor advise that I should leave off working, then I shall die;

And directly." At the age of seventy-eight, Martins attempted suicide by swallowing caustic soda. She died in the hospital three days later, on August 8, 1976. "I see everything through a mist," she wrote to J in her last letter. "The darkness is all around me."

Despite the tragic conditions of her death, Martins had a rare zest for living and a complete commitment to her art. On J's final visit to Martins, shortly before her death, J recalls asking her friend if she was afraid of dying. "Now, my darling," Martins responded, "when you get older you come to realize that *dying* isn't the problem. *Living* is the problem. That is why we must live our lives passionately and to the full. My agony would be to 'live dying' without being able to work."[3]

Helen Martins's artwork, once an object of derision from her local community, has become the single most important asset of the village of Nieu Bethesda. The artist is remembered for her distinct and explosive creativity. The Owl House was declared a national monument in 1989.

3

Seven years after visiting the Owl House, I was wandering through a retrospective on Georgia O'Keeffe at the Art Gallery of Ontario (AGO) when my thoughts returned to Helen Martins. It was a Wednesday night in late April, and I had just entered a crowded room when one painting caught my eye. I stopped to stare at what appeared to be the hills above my childhood village. When I drew closer, I could see I was mistaken. It wasn't the foothills of the Riviersonderend Mountains in the Little Karoo, but Cerro Pedernal, "Flint Hill," as seen from O'Keeffe's Ghost Ranch in northern New Mexico. I knew that here the shrub, or *fynbos*, had different names — elephant and salt grass, shaggy dropseed — and volcanic rock replaced the sandstone of my childhood terrain. Yet it was as if the artist had lifted the desert landscape directly from my sleeping brain and transcribed it to canvas.

I'd seen O'Keeffe's paintings online and in books, but this was the first time in the flesh. For the canvases felt like that, flesh. Her rippling purple hilltops looked like animal organs. "I have wanted to paint the desert and I haven't known how," O'Keeffe once wrote of her landscapes. "I always think that I cannot stay with it long enough … it is vast, empty, and untouchable — and knows no kindness with all its beauty."[4]

It was 2017. I'd just moved back to Canada to reshape my life, to funnel my intellectual ambition into the clear container of graduate school, even if it meant heartbreak. Like every immigrant, I think I was still searching for a place to call home but without really having a sense of what this word meant.

Drifting through the gallery on that April evening, I wasn't sure I'd made the right decision to return to Canada a second time. I often woke up in the morning not remembering where I was. It was a strange feeling. Similar to the one I had when we arrived in Canada on that first day when my siblings and I got lost on the tree-lined streets of our mountain town. This time it was worse, though. I didn't have my brother and sister by my side. I was older and less resilient. The apartment buildings in Montreal where I was living at the time all seemed too short. There was too much sky.

How can there be too much sky? It didn't make sense, but I felt exposed.

I think that this is why I felt so drawn to Georgia O'Keeffe, and why I'd travelled to Toronto to see the retrospective: She struck me as someone who could do just fine without human companionship. There was a romance to this self-sufficiency. A woman who had turned solitude — and even loneliness, which seemed like the less-dignified, less-creative cousin of solitude — into a landscape she could live in. And quite happily, it appeared. She was the lone figure on a hill, sublime in her individuated power. Unlike many of the other genius women I'd encountered (Sylvia Plath, Virginia Woolf, Lorraine Hansberry, Ana Mendieta, and even Helen Martins), her life had been long and not cut short by illness, depression, or jealous husbands. Her life, too, had been largely self-directed. That isn't to say her artistic trajectory was effortless. "It takes courage to be a painter," O'Keeffe once observed, "I always felt I walked on the edge of a knife. On this knife I might fall off on either side. But I'd walk it again. So what. So what if you do fall off? I'd rather be doing something I really wanted to do."[5]

I imagined this knife edge to be the volcanic line of Cerro Pedernal, the mountaintop where O'Keeffe's ashes were eventually scattered. Perhaps she could teach me to embrace my own aloneness and to be more courageous about it, to claim a world for myself.

It was only years later when reading O'Keeffe's biography that I realized, feeling a little deceived, that she was not the stern, solitary, and invulnerable icon I'd imagined her to be. Not exactly. She'd had a robust career in New York City, many good friends, and a husband/patron, and other artists had often visited her at her home in New Mexico.[6] O'Keeffe had also suffered anxiety attacks and depression, which she referred to as "long periods of uncertainties in my mind." There was one especially dark period in the 1930s. Unable to eat, sleep, or paint, she developed a fear of water and tall buildings and was eventually hospitalized for psychoneurosis.

Yet O'Keeffe always had a huge and admirable lust for life. In her letters to her friend and biographer, Anita Pollitzer, the painter wrote: "So few people live — they just seem to exist — and I don't see any good reason why we shouldn't *live always* — till we die physically — why do we do it all in our teens and twenties." In another letter, O'Keeffe added, "I haven't found anyone who likes to live like we do."[7] I'm reminded of Helen Martins's fear of having to "live dying," her insistence that life must be lived passionately and to the full.

In one of the rooms at the AGO, I encountered a painting of a low blue mountain range, animal bones rising up before it. The work was captioned *Pelvis with the Distance, 1943.* It must have been the emptiness of O'Keeffe's landscapes — of this blue distance circled by bone — that allowed me to project my past onto them. Here were the same burnt soil and scattered grasslands. The vast, unbroken sky. Quite by accident, O'Keeffe's landscapes unlocked a portal into my early memory. As I moved between gallery rooms, I felt I was walking into the past — toward my own desert origins. My visit to South Africa rushed back to me and, for a moment, I felt that I was standing again in Helen Martins's statue garden, under the desert sun.

Like Martins, O'Keeffe had also made sculptures of the materials from her environment: antlers, rocks, and bones. These sculptures surrounded me, illuminated in the gallery's yellow light, strange monuments casting precise shadows along the walls. They felt enduring, free of the obligation of representation.

I wrote in my notebook: "The soul must live in the bones. Where else would the soul live?" Now paging through this notebook, one of many slim, tan-coloured books I've kept over the years, I wonder if those sentences are my lines or O'Keeffe's.

Soon the gallery attendant would come to usher out the exhibition's last visitors, but for now, I was transfixed. I imagined myself to be back in the old century, my birth century, not quite in the rear-view mirror. If I squinted, I could just see her, the artist rising early before the heat. Was it O'Keeffe or Martins?

• • •

What had attracted me to Helen Martins's and Georgia O'Keeffe's stories of retreat? Was it the need for a model? Or an interest in feminist refusal — the rejection of the conventional life? Or was it simply curiosity, a need to understand what kind of art could be produced at this limit?

Two women making art in the desert in a time when women were not readily recognized as artists. Yet their creations were very different. Martins's sculptures were nothing like O'Keeffe's landscape paintings. Whereas O'Keeffe was careful never to include a human figure or a living animal, Martins's world was filled with people and mythical creatures, larger than life with glass-cut eyes. This throng of life may have been an attempt at shielding herself from the isolation of her desert town, of populating — even overpopulating — her environment. O'Keeffe's empty, figureless landscapes may have been a way to make more room for herself and her life within her marriage.

• • •

Around the time Helen Martins was obtaining her teaching diploma in Graaff-Reinet, Georgia O'Keeffe was teaching painting to students in West Texas. She didn't like teaching. She found that the job swallowed all her time and energy, leaving her with little left for her own painting. She complained that she was merely existing, not *living*. What she needed was a patron. Little did she know that she was about to find one and that they would become one of the most iconic artist couples of the twentieth century.

While in Texas, O'Keeffe sent some abstract charcoal drawings to her friend Anita Pollitzer in New York City, who without her knowledge, showed them to Alfred Stieglitz. Stieglitz was already a prominent photographer and gallery curator at this time. He regularly exhibited major European and American avant-garde artists, including several who have already wandered through this book: Rodin, Picasso, Braque, Cézanne, Matisse, and Duchamp.

"Finally a woman on paper!" Stieglitz exclaimed upon first seeing O'Keeffe's charcoal abstracts, which he later exhibited in his gallery.[8] Even before the dark-haired young woman walked into his gallery in New York in 1916, Stieglitz knew he'd met his muse and his equal — though O'Keeffe was twenty-four years his junior, he called her his "twin." He promptly divorced his wife, and a year later, O'Keeffe moved to New York to live with him and, more generally, to live with the art world that frequented his gallery.

This worked out well for them for some time. But eventually O'Keeffe began to feel stifled.[9] She had to make a change if she wanted to keep painting.

In 1929 she took the first of many trips to New Mexico, writing to Stieglitz: "There is much life in me — when it was always checked in moving toward you — I realized it would die if it could not move toward something.... I chose coming away because here at least I feel good, and it makes me feel I am growing very tall and straight inside, and very still." Stieglitz wrote back that he was devastated by her absence, but in her response, she reiterated her need for artistic growth through solitude and independence. "I have not wanted to be anything but kind to you — but there is nothing to be kind to you if I cannot be me — And me is something that reaches very far out into the world and all around."[10]

Though their marriage was rocked by power struggles and Stieglitz's infidelities and egotism, the couple seemed to have had an overall refreshingly honest relationship, especially for the time. There was more creative equality here than in the relationship between Helen Martins and her dramaturge husband, for instance, or Edward Hopper and Jo Nivison Hopper or perhaps even Gertrude Stein and Alice B. Toklas, for whom the boundaries of caretaker and genius were clearly delineated.

Walking through the AGO on that night in April, I wondered what it would have been like to live the way O'Keeffe had: to know your boundaries and define them. There is one photograph of her, taken by Yousuf Karsh, that beautifully captures her determination to grow "tall and straight inside." The artist is in her home in Abiquiú. She's sitting on a bench in a black suit jacket and skirt, a whorled stump beside her, above her, a crest of antlers. She faces the door, the light on the door frame not yet touching her.

It's easy to imagine her rising, exiting the photograph through this door, standing in the sunshine, gazing out over the flat valley, in its recesses, a dark purple hill. Pedernal. Again, the line from her letter to Anita Pollitzer comes to me: "I don't see any good reason why we shouldn't live always."

After her husband's death, O'Keeffe moved to New Mexico permanently. This is when she began to paint the sky through pelvic bones. The hole in the bone became a room, the body worn down to its essential map or set of instructions.

In another photograph of the artist in later life, O'Keeffe cuts a striking figure in black perched among the bleached stones and dark soil of her chosen landscape: a crow-like woman, talented, reclusive, highly productive. No wonder so many women writers and artists have fallen for Georgia O'Keeffe and have also claimed her as their muse and twin.

• • •

One gallery room held several variations of the purple mountain, Cerro Pedernal. Portraits in different weather, different light. "It is hazy — and my mountain floats out light blue in the distance — like a dream," O'Keeffe wrote. "It is my private mountain; it belongs to me. God told me if I painted it enough I could have it."[11]

I read these lines as an example of O'Keeffe's sense of humour. There's also a certain poetry in the idea that if you paint or write about a landscape enough, it becomes part of you: It belongs to you and you belong to it. At the same time, there was something uncomfortable about a visitor claiming ownership of a place, even if it was only symbolic ownership. Later, when considering these lines, assiduously copied down in my notebook, it was hard not to read this desire for possession as undergirded by a colonial impulse. Even if these lines were not intended that way, O'Keeffe was a settler artist. As Indigenous scholars have noted, because of the lasting influence of her art in the public imagination, Northern New Mexico in its entirety has been dubbed "O'Keeffe's Country," a term that excludes the original people who lived there. O'Keeffe was also part of an art community that included a number of notable artists and intellectuals who romanticized the desert, depicting the Southwest as a vast, empty, largely uninhabited space.[12] This emptiness celebrated the beauty of the land, but it also erased the presence of the communities that had lived there long before the art world "discovered" the place.

There was a similar impulse at work in the brochures and websites advertising the Karoo to tourists visiting South Africa. Karoo villages, or *dorpies*, like the one in which Helen Martins had lived, were filled with picture book churches and Cape Dutch houses with green-painted shutters, aloe blossoms, and wild rose vines. But outside many of these picturesque villages existed a shadow town, an informal settlement where the farm labourers and domestic workers lived in cheap housing or shacks built from corrugated metal. Historically, the official village and the unofficial settlements were divided along class and colour lines.

On my visit to the Karoo, I caught myself unconsciously framing my shots of the landscape to exclude the telephone wires, shacks, and trucks, to make the desert seem untouched by industry, out of time. Ahistorical. Perhaps I hoped to capture an image that resembled my memory of the land more closely than its reality. But no landscape exists outside history. There's always something the camera, or the painter's brush, doesn't see. There's always something the biographer leaves out.

• • •

The gallery was closing for the night. I pulled myself away from O'Keeffe's silent landscapes and walked through the city feeling how I often do after visiting a museum: that my life has, at least incrementally, been changed. The next time I returned to the AGO it would be for Anishinaabe artist Rebecca Belmore's *Facing the Monumental*, an exhibition on the tension between difficult subjects and beautiful aesthetics.

4

Looking back on photographs of the Camel Yard and the tiny sketch in my notebook of O'Keeffe's purple mountain, I'm reminded of what Ana Mendieta once said of her own earth works: "My art is the way I reestablish the bonds that unite me to the universe." This is what I see in the uplifted arms of the cement men and women in Martins's garden and what I see in O'Keeffe's bone landscapes — an attempt to renew that bond, to establish a lifeline to the universe.

I turned to these artists when I was trying to reestablish that bond for myself, in a time when I felt dislocated and floating. Solitude, it seemed to me, could be a form of self-care and protection; it could be nourishment. Isolation, on the other hand, whether in the desert or in the city, could prove destructive, as it eventually had for Martins. Yet the two states seemed hard to parse, their distinctions not always traceable. Perhaps this distinction was what I was searching for in my pilgrimage to their monuments, the Owl House in the Great Karoo and, years later, the landscapes and bone portraits in the AGO.

I no longer believed an artist could live solely in her paintbox. Ultimately, the lives and art of these two women in the desert convinced me of the importance of community in the artist's life. That one needed community in order to enjoy solitude; otherwise, that solitude turned to isolation.

I don't believe that Helen Martins lived solely in isolation. I recognize the "exalted feverishness" of the outsider artist in her sculptures — their originality even when depicting familiar allegorical, mythical, or religious figures, such as the three wise men, or the Easter Island statues — but I believe it was the small connections that she could make to the outside world (for instance, the friendship with J and the companionship of her assistants and collaborators) that kept her making art for as long as she did. Imagine if she could have broadened that community — islanded as she was in the beauty and hostility of her desert world — imagine if she could have joined a larger parade.

• • •

It was noon when I finally emerged from the Owl House, all those years ago, weaving my way back through the Camel Yard. Simon offered to drive me to the top of the nearby hill, which at this hour was cast in a purple shadow. From the lookout, the village shrank to the size of a sardine can, a small glistening thing surrounded by farms, dry open grassland, and sky. In the distance, I could just see the informal community, the shadow town, on the village outskirts. Simon also lived in a shadow town, the one just outside Graaff-Reinet. He offered to take me there on the way home to meet his family. He had two young kids who would love to meet a real-life Canadian, even if I was born in South Africa.

As we headed out of Nieu Bethesda, Simon and I drove past a small game reserve. Local animals, Simon explained in Afrikaans, slowing the taxi and pointing to a sign on the gate. Did I want to see? He got out and unhitched the gate. When he returned to the vehicle, he offered to switch places with me so that I would be in the driver's seat. But I couldn't drive, I tried to explain. He shook his head and gestured to the wheel.

He seemed amused that this was to be my first driving experience — in the middle of the Karoo bush, among wild animals.

White-chested monkeys crouched in the branches above us, impassively judging my poor driving skills as I lurched the car forward. Two kudu with giant curved horns grazed among the nearby sweet thorn bushes, gently tossing their heads to dislodge flies. They glanced up, but seemingly accustomed to visitors, they kept on tugging at the grass as we drove past, car jolting as I shifted gears. It seemed fitting that I should undergo this coming-of-age ritual in the country of my birth: the matriculation from child to adult, driver of her own destiny, though it would be more than a decade before I obtained my actual driver's licence.

Driving through this wild Eden on that afternoon in 2010, I couldn't stop thinking about the statues in Helen Martins's sculpture garden — that peculiar oasis in the desert that, for a moment, had extended its welcome to me. Even knowing now of the tragic circumstances around her death, I couldn't help but feel that her art had made my world bigger. The artist wasn't present, but I could still feel her stamina, her delight in her work, her determination to keep building her strange procession in the desert, against all odds.

Beyond the kudu, a herd of springbok drifted through the thorn bushes. From this distance, they appeared only half real, more dream-of-deer than deer. I imagined that they had hopped right out of the Camel Yard, out of the artist's mind, stone come to life.

10

A Record of Girlhood

I LEFT THE DESERT, TRAVELLING COASTWARD, TO MY grandmother's house. This would be the first time I'd meet my grandmother in my adult life. It would also be the last time, though I didn't know that yet. Exiting the Great Karoo, I headed south toward Durbanville, a suburb of Cape Town. As I watched the semi-desert shrubland flash past my bus window, I remembered what Virginia Woolf wrote about the maternal line, that a woman must think back through her mothers and grandmothers to write fiction. Woolf meant literary mothers, of course, but occasionally, I imagined my literary grandmothers and my biological grandmothers meeting. It was hard to picture the encounter, though, as I knew so little about my biological grandmothers. It's a strange position to be in — to know one's literary grandmothers better than one's biological grandmothers. With the exception of the first decade of my childhood, when we still lived in South Africa,

I'd grown up mostly grandmother-less. The main reason was geographical distance, but it was also social distance within my large and scattered family.

It made me uneasy, though, to have spent so much time researching women artists and feminist histories but virtually know nothing about my own bloodlines. Where were my own grandmothers in the history of women among monuments?

I don't have many memories of my paternal grandmother, Herma, who lived in another part of the country and who died when I was still a child, but in the ones I do have she's always presenting me with coins and candy, pressing my cheeks, eager to love me.

I have more memories of my grandmother on my mother's side, with whom I share my first name. "Kasia" is a Polish version of the Irish "Kathleen" and was a nickname given to my grandmother by her second husband, a Polish immigrant to South Africa. We knew him as Dziadzio, Grandpa, and her affectionately as Gaga, Grandma. They lived in a suburb outside Cape Town, and growing up, my brother, sister, and I often visited her, spending several nights at her house while my mother had appointments in the city. I remember the thick hedge around the entrance to her house, the upright piano in the entranceway. How we hugged her, formally, one by one, and then raced outside to her garden. In my memories, she lives alone in the house, Dziadzio having passed away when we were still very small. I remember, specifically, how she patted us dry us in a big white towel after our baths, softly chanting, "Rub a dub dub, three men in a tub, and who do you think they were? The butcher, the baker, the candlestick maker, all sailed to sea in a rotten potato." I imagined that we, my siblings and I, were the three men of the nursery rhyme, though none of those professions appealed to me, especially not the butcher. At the time, I'd have preferred to be a mermaid, or the sea itself.

In my M.A., I applied for the scholarship to return to South Africa largely because I was curious about this country that seemed to only exist in my past — a sun-warmed, vanished record of childhood. I almost believed that I'd step out the plane into my childhood, as if the first twelve years of my life existed, vacuum-sealed, in a vault under my old village.

During this visit, I gave my grandmother a copy of Alice Munro's story collection *The Progress of Love*.[1] It happened to be the book I was travelling with at the time, and I handed it to her, unwrapped, because I'd forgotten to bring her a proper gift. But what would I have brought her instead? Since I'd lived in Canada most of my life, we didn't know each other well. We were near-strangers who, in certain angles, shared a profile and slightly crooked teeth.

But perhaps I wanted my biological and literary grandmothers to meet even then. Because of my identification with Munro's narrators and my physical similarity to my grandmother, I wanted to think I resembled these two women and that they resembled each other. After all, they were around the same age. This was long before I — and much of the world — learned about Munro's betrayal of her daughter.

• • •

Alice Munro, the Nobel laureate and Canadian literary giant, died as I was writing this book in 2024. Two months after her death, her youngest daughter, Andrea Robin Skinner, publicly shared her story of her sexual abuse as a child at the hands of her stepfather, Munro's second husband, Gerald Fremlin.

Skinner wrote that she first told her mother about the abuse in 1992 when Skinner was in her twenties. Munro briefly left Fremlin but ultimately returned to him and stayed with him until his death.

"I also wanted this story, my story, to become part of the stories people tell about my mother," Andrea Skinner wrote. "I never wanted to see another interview, biography or event that didn't wrestle with the reality of what had happened to me, and with the fact that my mother, confronted with the truth of what had happened, chose to stay with, and protect, my abuser."[2]

For years, I'd wished my biological grandmother were more like my literary grandmother. Now I was heartsick for Andrea. I was shocked that the story of her abuse was only coming to light in 2024, even though Gerald Fremlin had been charged with indecent assault against Andrea and pleaded guilty in a 2005 trial. How had this open secret not made it into Munro's biography? How had it not made it into the media before now? The answer: because Munro was so famous, so cherished, because too many people's careers were at stake, because she was "Our Chekhov."

Yes, we were part of the reason, too. Because of our national claim to Munro's monument, to her role as our literary mother, her own daughter's story was suppressed.

Skinner's account recalls Linda's story, or the story of Picasso's adopted daughter, or Dylan Farrow's alleged abuse by Woody Allen. It conjures the gaze of the child on the horsehair sofa in Thomas Eakins's photograph. At the bottom of these archives of genius, another story of a harmed child.

• • •

When I gave my grandmother a copy of *The Progress of Love*, I was ignorant of Munro's personal life but felt that I knew her intimately based on her stories. Was my attraction to Munro, particularly her stories set in the postwar period of the 1950s and 1960s, driven in part by my hunger to know more about my grandmother's coming of age?

My grandmother and Munro were both of a generation of women that in Munro's words weren't young enough to really be with the "watershed decade for women" — the 1960s, which saw the rise of the second-wave feminist movement — but were "young enough to see that all possibilities were not closed to us." Even the syntax of this last sentence, the meaning inferred in the negative, signals how fragile these possibilities were understood to be. Access to the wider world is kept ajar by that small word *not*.

Did my grandmother see these possibilities? Was she interested in them? I recalled again Kate Chopin: "I would give up my life for my children; but I wouldn't give myself."

I knew so little about my grandmother. I knew that she'd given birth to ten children, and with the addition of four step-children, had raised fourteen — my mother eighth in the succession. I knew she kept an orderly house. That she remained faithful to the Catholic Church until her death.

• • •

When I arrived at her house, my grandmother was not as I remembered her. She'd grown very thin, frail, and birdlike, which was strange, since she'd always been a sturdy woman, broad-shouldered in her cardigans and boxy floral dresses, almost Gertrude Stein–like in her countenance. Her gaze was still sharp but no longer focused on the people and objects around her. She seemed alert to something beyond the reality of the room, the car (with my uncle in the driver's seat, me in the back), or even to the restaurant where we ate lunch.

This restaurant stood at the entrance of Kirstenbosch National Botanical Garden, directly beneath Table Mountain and the Skeleton Gorge. It's probably my favourite place in the city because of the memories I have of going there as a child, wandering the herb gardens for the blind, smelling my way along the paths with my eyes shut. Or lingering in the Protea Garden where the flowers bore a soft white fuzz. In the restaurant, we ordered scones, strawberry jam, and clotted cream. The menu was still securely anchored in colonial times, like the monument to Cecil John Rhodes in his three-piece suit still standing and not yet covered up at the time. The three of us sat around a small table overlooking the gardens. My grandmother hardly touched food now; it was as if she was already departing, living on weak black tea and milk. She didn't say much, letting me and my uncle carry the conversation. But she seemed content to be out in the winter sunlight. We took a photo of the three of us before we left the gardens. My uncle and I appear like giants beside her.

After we drove home from the restaurant, she and I sat in her cool, dimly lit living room with the vertical blinds that divided up the front garden. There were many large sofas in this room — more than she could possibly use, since she lived alone in the house and rarely had visitors. The unused floral-print sofas and overstuffed chairs seemed to take on personalities of their own. I imagined them to be low-rent lodgers lounging about the room, watching me expectantly.

The lawn outside was yellowing in the winter sun; it hadn't rained in months. The garden had been well maintained for thirty years, but the gardener, Daniel, had retired and gone to live with his family in the northeast. The garden remained tidy, but there was a sense of it having faded, past its prime, of no longer being loved. Looking out at the lawn, I remembered playing among the hedgerows as a child, hiding beneath their furry silver leaves, sage, and lamb's ears, or chasing my brother and sister along the path that ran beside the garden's outer limit and was shaded by squat, dark-leaved trees and the tight hoops of the fence.

I wasn't quite sure if my grandmother knew who I was. I was talking too much to fill in the silence, which seemed heavier now that the blinds were half drawn. I told her I'd received a scholarship to a graduate program and had won a small literary prize. I didn't think she was listening to me — after all, she'd had a lifetime of babies and adult children demanding her attention, trying to impress her with their accolades — but she leaned forward to take a look at my paperback copy of *The Progress of Love*, which I had set on the coffee table.

After my grandmother's death a few years later, her caregiver told me that during her final months, she'd read *The Progress of Love* over and over again. From start to finish.

• • •

Like many of Alice Munro's stories, my favourite in *The Progress of Love* tells of a young mother trying to balance domestic labour with intellectual ambition and feeling guilty about it. Set in 1961, "Miles City, Montana" follows a suburban family's cross-country road trip and contains all the expected trials of such an endeavour — the hot car, irritable children, a strained marital debate about the importance of lettuce on sandwiches, as well as an unexpected one, the near-drowning of the narrator's youngest daughter in an unattended public swimming pool in Miles City. The narrator, a restless, unfulfilled housewife, is closely aligned with Munro herself — in fact, her biographer, Robert Thacker, captioned a photograph of the author and her two young daughters on the West Coast: "Jenny, Alice, and Sheila Munro, Vancouver, July 1961, the summer of the 'Miles City, Montana' trip." Her eldest daughter, Sheila, also recalls the trip. This was before Andrea was born, and years before Munro left her first marriage.

It's easy to read Munro's tight smile and faraway, vaguely agitated gaze in this photograph as belonging to the narrator. She could be the dark-haired housewife whose husband frequently commands her and the children to pose for the camera, exclaiming, "Great. You look like Jackie Kennedy!" Judging from autobiographical accounts and interviews, Munro did harbour the same desires as the housewife in "Miles City, Montana" — the wish for privacy, uninterrupted time, and movement beyond the domestic sphere. As the housewife/narrator reflects:

> In my own house, I seemed to be often looking for a place to hide — sometimes from the children but more often from the jobs to be done and the phone ringing and the sociability of the neighborhood. I wanted to hide so that I could get busy at my real work, which was a sort of wooing of distant parts of myself. I lived in a state of siege, always losing just what I wanted to hold on to.[3]

Although a continent and hemisphere separated my grandmother from the Canadian landscapes in which most of Munro's stories take place, both my grandmother and Munro were born into the British colonial empire. Both were settlers. And though both experienced the patriarchal constraints of the 1950s as young mothers and housewives, both were relatively educated and privileged. I wondered if my grandmother recognized herself in Munro's stories. Many of them are about motherhood, specifically the struggle to reconcile the role of carer with that of artist. Or perhaps it was that she didn't recognize herself — and this is what returned her again and again to the stories. Or was it just that she had so few books in her house that this one presented to her an escape or distraction as she awaited death? Some years earlier, she'd told my mother that all her friends had died, all the women she used to sing with in her church choir. Now she was just waiting.

At the time I gifted *The Progress of Love* to my grandmother, I identified with Munro's girls and women. I believed I was Del, the narrator in *Lives of Girls and Women*, whose restless ambition but simultaneous desire for conventionality disturb the social equilibrium of her rural community. I believed I was Juliet in the linked stories in *Runaway* who, when visiting her parents in their small Canadian town, is subtly punished for her "odd" life choices — that is, her choice to pursue a Ph.D. in classics. "Odd choices were simply easier for men," remarks Juliet, "most of whom would find women glad to marry them."[4] I'd felt the same way at various points in my life.

Maybe my grandmother didn't relate to those characters in the same way, having made fewer odd choices than I, but I wondered if she felt some of their frustrations.

Then again, Juliet does meet a dashing stranger on a cross-country train, played by Daniel Grao in *Julieta*, Pedro Almodóvar's adaptation of the three linked stories "Chance," "Soon," and "Silence," and Juliet eventually settles down with the stranger on the train on the West Coast of Canada.

Although Juliet suspects him of being chronically unfaithful to her, they have a daughter together, a life.

One day, after an argument, Juliet's lover goes fishing and drowns in a storm. Juliet becomes a widow. In the final story in the cycle, we see that she has become estranged from her adult daughter as well.

The true heartbreak of the story exists here, not in the death of the lover but in the loss of the daughter, who is raising her family in another part of Canada and has cut all communication with her mother without explaining why. I always found this odd — that there was no explanation for this separation, that the mother figure would spend the rest of her life trying to understand what she did wrong. What she did to deserve this silence from her daughter.

Of this longing for the lost daughter, Munro writes:

> Whenever she came in, the first thing Juliet did was look for the light flashing on her answering machine.... She tried various silly tricks, to do with how many steps she took to the phone, how she picked it up, how she breathed. *Let it be her.*
>
> Nothing worked.[5]

One day in Vancouver Juliet bumps into one of her daughter's school friends who doesn't know of the estrangement. Coincidentally, the friend had just run into Penelope and her family in Edmonton, Alberta. Juliet learns that Penelope has five children. She's overcome by this news. Until this encounter with her daughter's school friend, Juliet had no knowledge that she, Juliet, was a grandmother.

When I first read the Juliet stories, I remember thinking the heartbreak in the final story felt so real. In the biographical accounts I'd read, Munro was close with her daughters. It was a sign of Munro's emotional genius that she could write so convincingly about what I determined must be an unlived experience of grief. And yet it felt so true. It was only in the summer of 2024, when reading Andrea's account of her life with (and without) Munro, that I realized this story of estrangement was based on autobiographical material — the arc of her own life. The difference is that in the real-life version of events, there's no question why the daughter has made her life elsewhere, away from her mother, away from the harm of her mother's house.

In the last paragraph of "Silence," the final story in the Juliet series in *Runaway*, the narrative shifts from past tense to present. We're told that Juliet "keeps on hoping for a word from Penelope, but not in any strenuous way. She hopes as people who know better hope for undeserved blessings, spontaneous remissions, things of that sort."[6]

I think this shift to present tense is important. It reveals the ongoing nature of grief. Of longing for answers to the unanswerable questions we're left with as we grapple with Munro's legacy. And with the great silence we're left with after her death.

• • •

On the day before I left Cape Town, my grandmother and I were sitting in my uncle's car. We were on our way to a restaurant for my farewell dinner. My uncle left the car running as he popped into the corner store. While he was out of the car, my grandmother turned around to look at me in the back seat. Her pale blue eyes lucid for a moment, she searched my face.

"Do you have a boyfriend?" she asked. I didn't answer at first. Was this simple curiosity or was she worried that I wasn't on the right track, meaning on the track to the good life: marriage, children, security? Was she asking: Are you happy? Are you alone? Are you free?

"No," I said, feeling as if I'd failed her.

I didn't know very much about my grandmother's girlhood, but when I asked my mother about it, I was surprised to discover that her biography had taken an uncannily similar turn to Juliet's story in "Chance." Kathleen had also met her future husband on a train, though this one was travelling from Zimbabwe (then Rhodesia), where her parents lived, to Cape Town, where she boarded at a convent.

This is how I imagine their meet-cute in a film adaptation, preferably also directed by Pedro Almodóvar: The scene opens on a girl in a train berth brushing her hair, which is long and honey-coloured and requires a hundred strokes of the brush per day. The berth door swings open as the train jolts along. Enter Launcelot Edwards, a young engineer on the way home to Cape Town to help his parents run their hotel. He happens to be passing along the train's corridor just as the berth door swings aside, revealing young Kathleen in all her Pre-Raphaelite glory. Eyes meet. Light on rippling hair. The train lurches. Launce almost loses his footing. Muttered apologies, both his and hers, as she jumps up to close the berth door.

Later in the dining car, he introduces himself to her. Tells her he's a land surveyor, that he hopes to buy a farm, a big house to hold a big family. Kathleen listens carefully to this earnest young man, her hair now tightly fixed in two long braids.

• • •

My grandmother has no written record of her life, with the exception of one diary, a gift from her youngest daughter on her eightieth birthday. My aunt had presented her with the notebook, blank except for the occasional inspirational quote, and asked her to describe her life's passage. It wasn't a diary then so much as a brief scan of a life lived largely off the record.

The country my grandmother was born in no longer exists; she was married before finishing high school, outlived two husbands, raised fourteen children, and saw the rise and fall of South Africa's apartheid system. These are the central details. But what she chose to describe instead in this record, the only one she was to produce of her life, were the homes she lived in.

Her earliest memories were of the front and side views of her childhood home, a bungalow built on stilts on Livingstone Avenue in Salisbury, now Harare, Zimbabwe. It's a strange feeling, tracing this colonial legacy through her architectural sketches. I'm immediately transported into a world of khaki-clad officers, women in wide summer hats and white dresses, a tremor of heat and banality and violence undergirding everything: the buildings, roads, teacups, piano lessons.

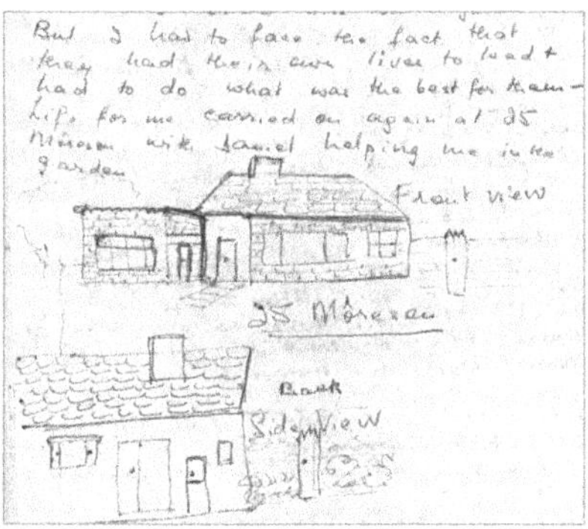

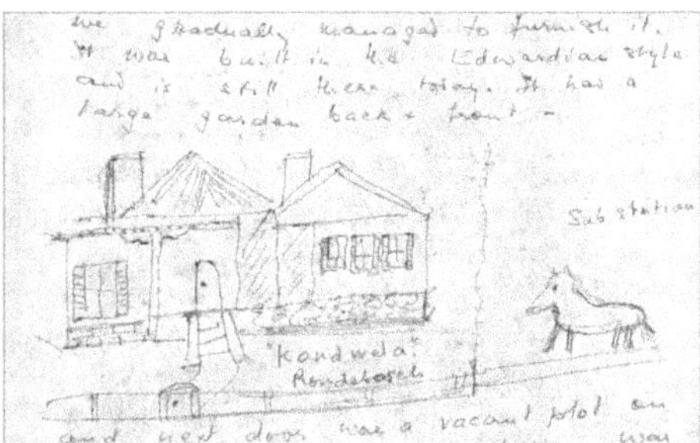

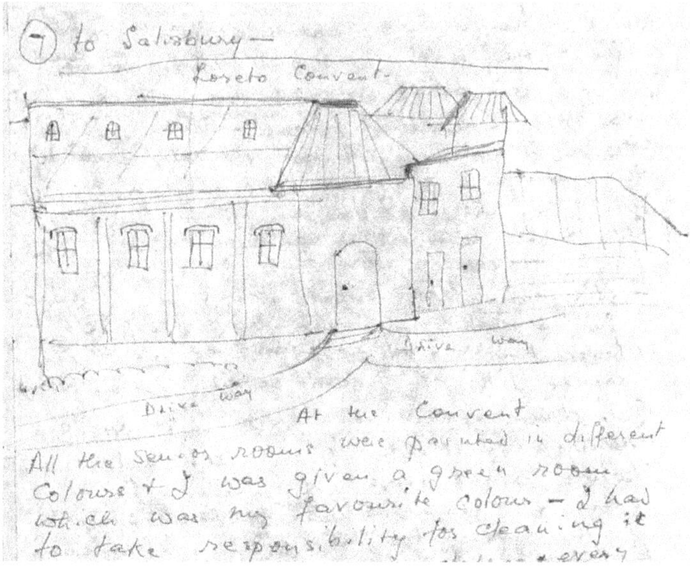

• • •

"We look at the world once, in childhood / The rest is memory."[7] Louise Glück's lines from her poem "Nostos" haunt me as I follow the story of my grandmother's girlhood, which takes up much of her notebook. She sketched the driveway of the Cape Town Loreto Convent where she boarded as a schoolgirl and where the Catholic nuns took protective, even obsessive, pride in her. This is where, she explains, she had to learn to do domestic work that had once been done by the servants in her childhood home. This is where I learn she once had servants.

Beneath her sketch of the convent, she writes:

> At the convent all the senior rooms were painted in different colours and I was given a

> green room which was my favourite colour —
> I had to take responsibility for cleaning it and
> for the state of my clothes and every Saturday
> was inspection day when we also washed our
> hair and mended our clothes if necessary.

These are the skills she brought to her marriage, to her career in motherhood. This is where I learn that her favourite colour is green.

• • •

I think I wanted my grandmother to be more like Alice Munro, to be artistically ambitious and frustrated with her role as maker and keeper of the home and children. To be discouraged with the convent and its controlling sisters, not admiring them. I saw her as someone following her duty — to the Catholic faith to produce a seemingly limitless stream of children, and to the 1950s social norms that exempted her from a professional life. But I imagined that secretly she yearned for something beyond the babies and the foaming dishpans. I thought I might find evidence of a nascent feminist agitation in my grandmother's notebook. After all, the rebellious spirit ran in our family. Her own mother, Kathleen Attracta, had escaped Ireland and a life of servitude to her brothers.

Leafing through my grandmother's sketches of houses, empty driveways hedged by subtle grey plants with petal-less flowers, traced from a memory reaching seventy-five years into the past, I was struck by how important the home, as an idea, a physical space, a feeling, had been to her and to so many women of her generation. There were the dwellings she came to inhabit as a young bride, as a mother, as a widow, as a bride again, and a widow again. These rooms defined not only my grandmother's position in the world but also her way of perceiving the chronology of her life.

My grandmother's notebook moved me to think about how our living spaces continue to exist within memory, suspending, or dilating, or collapsing time. How in all these years, while power changes hands, while the new rules of citizenship are established, new flags sewn, these domestic interiors, the tablecloths and frosted glass, the ironing boards decked in heavy afternoon light are impressed, fossil-like, on the mind. More so than the Catholic Church, the rooms she had lived in had become the monuments she lived by.

To answer this book's inciting question: Where are the women? They were in these rooms — or rooms less comfortable than these — tending to the family.

My grandmother was a maker of rooms. Last time I visited her home, I stayed in one of these rooms. The bed had been made up the way I remember from childhood, with a fitted sheet and brown blanket. Utilitarian, tidy. But there was a vase of freshly picked flowers on the table beside the door. I see her sprinkling white sugar on our orange halves at breakfast. The oranges are always followed by cereal in bowls patterned with brown petals and vines, along with milk, and juice in tall plastic containers. There are wooden placemats with illustrations of waterfowl. A vast polished table once set for sixteen. Now there are only two of us.

I think about all the small acts of care that went into making these rooms, to maintaining the lives that filled these rooms, and think of Helen Martins's house, now a museum. When does the home become a museum and the museum a home?

• • •

I mentioned there was a train involved in my grandparents' courtship. My grandmother's mother, Kathleen Attracta Morris, and Launce's mother, Mrs. Edwards, were acquaintances. After the summer holidays, Mrs. Morris asked Mrs. Edwards to chaperone her daughter, Kathleen, on her six-day train journey from Rhodesia (now Zimbabwe) to the Loreto Convent in Sea Point, Cape Town, in South Africa. There might have been a glimmer of mermaid's hair through the train berth door but, officially, my grandparents' meeting took place because their mothers belonged to the same church. Unlike Juliet's train journey, theirs was strictly chaperoned.

It is in the description of my grandfather's courtship, conducted at the Loreto Convent, that my grandmother comes closest to recounting a sense of mislaid ambition. She describes herself as "a typical schoolgirl with long blonde plaits and full of the joys of life, taking most things in my stride," and her suitor as a worldly young man with degrees in civil engineering and land surveying from the University of Cape Town, who had travelled through Europe and worked on a mine in Rhodesia. She writes:

> He seemed to take a liking to me. Especially to my long hair — waist length — which I had to brush + plait daily. He offered to walk with me to Saint Michaels for Sunday Mass and told me later, that was when he first became attracted to me. I, at that stage, was more interested in school than romance + was keen to get back to school life and my friends. Launce asked if he could come to see me sometimes if the Superior would allow him.
>
> To my surprise — she did.

It was the Irish connection — Launce's mother being Irish and Catholic — that influenced the Mother Superior. But when the Mother Superior realized Launce had become, in Kathleen's words, "*too* serious and a distraction as far as my matric studies were concerned and also my future," she suggested that Kathleen's parents transfer their daughter to Hillcrest Convent, near Pretoria, fifteen hundred kilometres away, where Kathleen could finish her high school studies undisturbed. "This was duly arranged," writes Kathleen:

> So at the beginning of 1940, after the summer holidays in Rhodesia, I started it at Hillcrest. It was a big change for me — with new teachers, different set books in Latin, French, maths etc and having to make new friends.... I managed to settle down + became very friendly with the head girl Binks Keneally + vice head Dottie Dawson. I spent the Easter holidays with the Dawson family in a happy-go-lucky but academic atmosphere. The mother was a teacher + the father in charge of the agricultural experimental station outside Pretoria. I was still receiving long letters from Launce which, of course, intrigued, especially Binks. I eventually told her about him and also how I felt that he was fascinated with my long hair and didn't really know me as a person. Jokingly I said I feel like cutting off my plaits. Her reply was "Why don't you. You could cut one and I'll cut the other." I wrote to Launce + told him what I

> had done. He *was* very disappointed, but he didn't change his mind about me.

It's curious to me that she describes herself as "more interested in school than romance." I couldn't say the same thing for myself at seventeen. Did I infer a wistfulness in Kathleen's description of the academic atmosphere of her friend's household where both parents had professions? Also a whiff of apprehension in her concern that her suitor "didn't really know me as a person"? I wondered how many people had known her as a person in her own right, instead of as a caretaker or family matriarch.

• • •

En route to spend the June holidays with her parents in Hermanus, a popular vacation seaside town on South Africa's east coast, seventeen-year-old Kathleen is surprised at the Cape Town train station by Launce, who had arranged with her parents to drive her to Hermanus by car. They stop at a small restaurant at Kuils River called Halfway House where Launce produces an engagement ring:

> I was somewhat overawed, flattered and very confused in my feelings, and worried about my matric exams. I also had been thinking about the coming year and was leaning towards nursing as a career but I hadn't discussed things seriously with anyone. Launce had of course previously spoken to my parents and asked them to allow me to marry him as soon as possible. Their answer was "definitely not

> till I was 18." They should have insisted "not
> till after my matric exams."

Looking back, she writes: "I seem to be in a dream world, carried along by his insistence. And so my schooling came to an end."

• • •

At eighteen, I was backpacking across New Zealand with a woman who played the didgeridoo. We slept beneath volcanoes, on black sand beaches, in botanical gardens and abandoned apple orchards; we canoed with wild seals and swam in the Pacific at night, our arms and legs glowing with phosphorescence. During this time, I wrote every day, poems and stories, descriptions of the people and animals I met, the farms we worked on. We were broke; we had so much free time. I'd never have that amount of time again — the feeling of life, so huge and spontaneous, reeling out before me. Time without end.

I still have those journals somewhere. And maybe it was because I wrote so much in those late teenage years that I remember so clearly the feeling that my life was beginning. In Virginia Woolf's words, I was ready to "break into my hoard of life."[8] I see my grandmother at seventeen, about to break into her hoard of life, not sure what she will find there, not sure this hoard belongs to her. But perhaps that's my projection.

"I seem to be in a dream world, carried along by his insistence."

As I copy out my grandmother's passages, I'm tempted to edit her work. To bare down on the ambivalences, to root out an epiphany. Turn my grandmother into an Alice Munro heroine, full of guilt, frustration, and self-doubt. I want to end the description of my grandparents' courtship here, with the abrupt end of her education, the thing I've valued most in my life, to make a point about women's limited opportunities in the mid-twentieth century. But that wouldn't be fair to my grandmother. I must include her final phrase, written in handwriting uncannily similar to my mother's and to my own. It's a phrase that separates my grandmother and me: It reveals how different our trajectories would be.

"I spent the next few months preparing for marriage," she writes, "which for me was a big adventure."

• • •

What if I were to fall through time, just for one afternoon, and we were to meet on a train, my grandmother and me? Two light-haired young women in a passenger car. What would we say to each other?

I'd ask her about school, about what subjects she was studying. *Latin.* What sheet music she was currently learning on the piano. The only song I remember her playing was "Moonlight Sonata," and even then I don't recall seeing her play, even when I try to picture her at the upright piano in the foyer of her house in Durbanville.

I'd like to think we would have spoken about our mutual love of the St James Tidal Pool in Cape Town — that was somewhere she continued to visit in her old age. I'd tell her about the large chocolate-coloured dam in the Karoo where, as a young child, I learned how to swim. We'd order tea, play Scrabble like two Enid Blyton characters, or two young ladies from an Agatha Christie novel, set aboard a continental express in the 1930s. She'd beat me, since I've never had the mathematical mind required for board games. I've always been too interested in the words on the Scrabble board to be able to plot out a high numerical score. But my girl-grandmother was more scientifically inclined — after all, at one point she'd had ambitions to be a nurse.

I can see her now grinning at me and reaching into her bag to pull out a pair of sewing scissors. She hands me one of her long braids, which she's been tending to since childhood. "You could cut one and I'll cut the other." That's how girls show each other trust. Take my hair, transform me. Make me new.

Together, we fling our shorn clippings out the train window, watch them fly, souvenirs of girlhood, out into the desert.

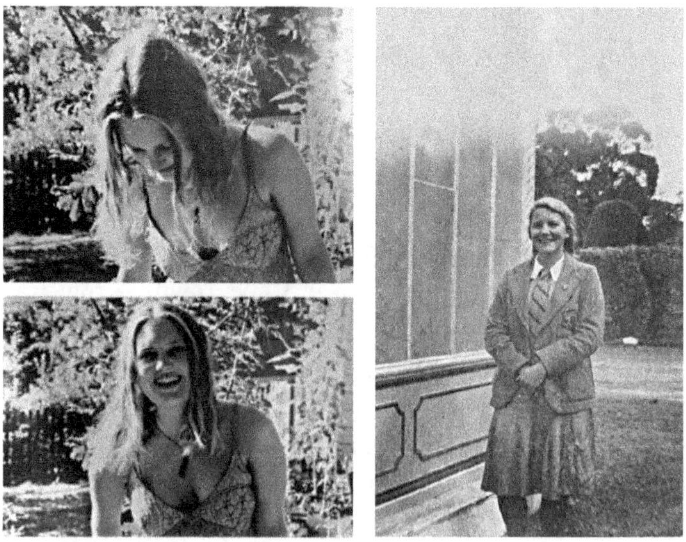

Me (left) and my grandmother (right) at seventeen years old.

11

The Artist's City

In the future will you chance the cold water of a body?

— T. Liem, *Slows: Twice*

When I think of revolution, I imagine it as a series of small, courageous, flawed attempts to risk everything.

— River Halen, *Dream Rooms*

1

I ARRIVED ON THE ISLAND EARLY. THE EMAIL WARNED THAT ferries filled up quickly this time of year and there was no guarantee of getting to the island dock for the 2:00 p.m. pickup. The bus, which only runs once a day, wouldn't wait for latecomers. I pulled my rolling suitcase into the shade and watched the passengers disembark. It was Monday, late August; school wasn't yet in session, but still I was surprised by the crowd. Teenagers exited the ferry on rusty bikes, with unicorns, yellow ducks, and enormous inflatable hot dogs under their arms. They disappeared down a road leading to the marina. Impeccably quaffed, golden-chested men, striped beach umbrellas and coolers in tow, headed toward the nude beach at Hanlan's Point. They were followed by tourists in white Oxford shirts, slightly dazed from the sun and only vaguely aware they'd taken the wrong ferry, for this was the wild part of the island, far away from the amusement park and the restaurants, and the little wooden village where the locals lived.

Two other passengers remained behind on the landing dock. Like me, they pulled their bags into the shade and watched the ferry head back to the city. Neither of the two passengers was carrying canvases or paints, so I concluded they must be writers. We waited in our solitary patches of shade before I broke the silence by introducing myself and asking them if they were also waiting for the pickup. They looked over at me with impassive faces, and I was reminded of the first day of university when I knew no one and felt like an imposter. I thought it would go away, this feeling, but even though I'd published a book the previous year, even though I'd dedicated my life to the study of books, I still often felt like an imposter in writers' circles. But then they nodded. One of the writers, tall and copper-haired, smiled and introduced herself as Harriet. She was a novelist. The other, a poet with round glasses and army-green overalls, said we could call her Dee.

"I came early because I thought I might miss the ferry," said Harriet. She told us she had a ten-month-old baby at home. This was the first time she was away from him. She was hoping to finish her book during her week on the island.

Dee was a civil servant. She planned to write a crown of sonnets while at the residency and had tasked herself with writing a poem each day. If she could do that, she'd be satisfied.

The next ferry arrived bearing more artists. There was Camille, a collage artist, who disembarked with a cargo bike loaded with paintbrushes, glue sticks, and a bushel of collard greens. Boris, tall and laconic, carried only a slim backpack, a sketchbook, and a single pair of clothes. Then there were the Timothies, who both lived in the city and were veterans of the island. Gen Z Timothy was an aspiring filmmaker, come to the island to finish a script. Millennial Timothy, or Timothy Senior, was an illustrator and the only full-time artist among us. The rest of us all had a secondary job. I was a sessional instructor at a university; Camille, a therapist.

Timothy Senior told me he'd been returning to the island for years. Sometimes even in the wintertime. It was desolate and beautiful in the winter, he said. Ice floating in the water. No one around. You got a lot done.

Just as we were introducing ourselves, our ride materialized, as if by collective thought, crawling along the winding, tree-lined road to the ferry launch.

"There's the 619," said Boris. "On time."

The 619 was an old 1970s school bus, powder blue with high ceilings, the kind people convert into tiny homes. In the driver's seat sat an older man in faded denim and a sun-bleached cap. He cut the engine and gazed at us through the open door. He had the still face of someone who has spent his life beside water and doesn't owe the dry world any explanation. Above the cab, written in block letters, our destination: ARTSCAPE, GIBRALTAR POINT. I thought the bus was empty until the doors opened and a slim bald man leaped down the steps with a clipboard clutched to his chest. He was Julian, the Artscape coordinator, here to welcome us and deliver us to our destination. He took our names and showed us where to load our luggage, wagons, and art supplies.

There was still one missing artist, but after a few minutes, the driver started the engine. I remembered the warning in the email: "The bus waits for no one." Julian conferred briefly with the driver and then shook his head. He glanced back at us, and it occurred to me that he seemed nervous. Was it because we were missing a member, or was it something else? We drove alongside the marina and past the old lighthouse. Julian told us that the residency building had once been an elementary school and also a wilderness education centre for children from the city. The classrooms were converted into studios in 1999, and the space had hosted visiting and long-term artists ever since. The residents slept in former offices and classrooms. He seemed to want to say more but stopped himself and instead stared out the window at the flashes of blue water between the trees.

When we arrived at the residency, a weathered, single-storey building set just off the road, we were instructed to drop off our bags in the hallway and meet in the huge central kitchen where we'd be given our keys and instructions for our stay.

Before heading to the kitchen, I peeled off from the group to survey the space. The building was sinking into the earth, its windows thick with cobwebs and dappled undersea light. I pressed through a white door into a huge ballroom, unfurnished except for a fireplace and a piano, with a sheet of windows looking out onto tangled vines, billowing hedges, and dry summer grass. A glass door opened onto a lawn, a firepit, and an informal path that led to what appeared to be a hole in the hedge. I followed the path to the hole, which like a Georgia O'Keeffe painting, opened to an emptiness so blue that I couldn't tell if it was water or sky. I felt as if I'd walked back through time and into a well-organized 1970s commune facing the sea, for right beyond the opening in the shrub hedge was the southernmost tip of the island, Gibraltar Point Beach. I knew there was another side to the lake and that the vague horizon almost visible through the blue haze contained another country. But it was easy to believe that I'd arrived at the edge of the world.

Someone was calling my name. Camille emerged from the bushes behind me. "It's stunning, isn't it?" she said, joining me at the opening in the hedge. "We're wanted in the kitchen. Julian has some kind of announcement to make. He told me to come find you."

Back in the kitchen, I knew something was wrong. Everyone was sitting around the table in a state of shock. The Timothies gazed at each other wide-eyed. Harriet was frowning. "What does this mean?" she asked.

"It means," said Julian, "that we're done. Twenty-four years and it's over, just like that."

"What's over?" asked Camille.

"The residency is closing down," said Boris, filling us in.

Artscape, the program offering the residency, had declared bankruptcy, and as of that morning, had fallen into receivership.[1] It wasn't just the island residency. Artscape had spaces across Toronto, including subsidized studios and housing for artists. This was a crisis on a grand scale. Julian told us we could stay for the night but that we might have to leave the next morning without notice and forfeit the rest of our residency. Most of the staff, including himself, had been let go. He would no longer be employed as of 5:00 p.m. Julian said he didn't have any further information but that we could stay at the residency tonight, since it was too late to try to find other accommodations. He handed us our keys.

This news had a rallying effect on our group. That evening, after Julian and the rest of the staff packed up their belongings and left, we sat around the kitchen table conspiring late into the night on how we might squat on the premises and live communally in the schoolhouse with its out-of-tune pianos and sinking floors, its blowing gardens of kale. We could live here forever, we decided, or at least until the Hanlan's ferry stopped operating for the winter.

"I'm not leaving," said Gen Z Timothy. He volunteered to go into the city in the morning and make copies of the existing keys in case the authorities tried to take them away and lock us out. But the next morning no one arrived to kick us out. No staff came, either, so we were alone at the residency — stowaways on an abandoned ship. I noticed that the 619 bus had a FOR SALE sign in its window. The Artscape ecosystem was disbanding.

Since no one showed up to evict us, we decided to make the most of our visit. That morning, and the following ones, we formed a collective ritual: All the artists migrated to the beach, some writing or drawing in notebooks, others building sculptures out of stones and driftwood. The sonneteer walked along the stretch of shore, disappearing around the bend and only returning an hour later, skin glistening. I swam laps, moving like an airplane over a planet of river grass until my face and finger bones ached from the cold. Camille joined me, resurfacing occasionally to shake out her long black hair. She seemed to be following a pattern: Every ten steps, she'd dive below the surface, then reappear metres away, then wade another ten steps along the island's shore. We spent the afternoons working in our studios, only reappearing at suppertime. Some continued to paint or collage or write through the night.

I spent my afternoons writing in a small room whose window was covered in heavy vines. Only little glimmers of light made it through the meshes of foliage, and I was reminded of the fairy tale my mother read to me as a child in which the princess pricks her finger on a spindle and everyone in the castle falls asleep for a hundred years. I could hear my mother's voice:

> The horses fell asleep in their stalls, the dogs in the courtyard, the pigeons on the roof, the flies on the walls, and even the fire on the hearth flickered, stopped moving, and fell asleep. The wind stopped blowing, and outside the castle not a leaf was stirring in the trees.

This was what those weeks on the island felt like — being magically suspended in time in a moment of crisis. There were dozens of rusty bikes chained up around the premises; they appeared to have been abandoned for a century. There were the wild gardens, the ballroom with its silent piano. I didn't want the spell to break, though I knew it was already broken.

In the evening, we gathered in the kitchen to prepare our remaining rations for dinner, for there were no grocery stores on the island. No convenience stores, either. Everything had to be ferried in from the city, which seemed to be located on another continent, unseen from this point of the island, even though its light still washed over us, blurring the stars at night.

I liked being separated from Toronto's conveniences — living in inconvenience changed my habits. With the city behind us, hidden by the island's trees, the artist residence offered a kind of nearness to the wild. Outside, in the old courtyard, a battalion of sunflowers saluted the sky. In the garden sprouted pockets of basil, stinging nettles, and stalks of purple corn, whose kernels turned out to be as hard and inedible as beads. Plums melted into the path leading to the greenhouse where we hung our wet beach towels after swimming, and our laundry on rainy days.

For several days, we waited for the authorities to arrive and expel us. In the meantime, as news of the receivership spread across the city, paintings started disappearing off the walls — former residents returning to take back their work before the banks came to claim the building. Many people came out from the city to see this mythic place before it vanished. A photographer friend of mine brought his camera, documenting the gardens and industrial hallways that served as exhibition spaces and contained all sorts of objects — Victorian baby carriages, curio cabinets, a small lending library, and yes, a spindle.

In the end, a compromise was struck, and we, the resident artists and writers, were given permission to stay at the schoolhouse until the end of our planned residencies, but the conspiratorial atmosphere remained. The closure of this, one of the last major artists residencies in Canada, prompted conversations about other shutdowns. Affordable artist housing and studios lost to corporate schemes. Small presses that had gone under; literary prizes and other forms of artist support that had lost their funding and had, in recent years, sunk into the murk of late-stage capitalism. And Toronto's creeping rents, which were squeezing everyone dry — this was a topic of conversation that rose up at least once a day. I had left Toronto for Montreal partially for this reason: I couldn't figure out how to live as a writer there. This was a hard task in any major city. As Toronto went the way of Vancouver, San Francisco, and New York City, I had bowed out.

"How do you survive?" I asked the other artists one night. Timothy Senior had opened a bottle of gin, and we were improvising cocktails with sprigs of mint from the garden. "On a day-to-day basis, how do you manage to feed yourself and also make art?"

Boris shrugged. "I shoplift. Couple times a week."

He clarified that he only shoplifted from major corporate stores. Loblaws, for example, which was owned by the wealthiest family in Canada and was known for avoiding taxes via offshore investment vehicles, fixing the price of bread, and fighting employees' potential to earn a livable wage at every turn.[2] Since 2019, Boris explained, the company had generated a compounded annual growth rate of 13.9 percent on top-line revenue, while averaging over 30 percent gross margins.[3] But what was truly odious was this: During the pandemic, as consumers struggled to pay for food, the company generated a compounded annual growth rate of 31.7 percent on net income. It profited off the crisis.

When he shopped at Loblaws, Boris made an effort to shoplift at least 30 percent of his groceries — 30 to 40 percent was ideal. This was to offset the growth profits of Loblaws. When I asked him how he managed to shoplift without being detected, he showed me his technique, which involved several ingenious steps and some sleight of hand, which I won't divulge here.

The other artists at the table didn't seem surprised.

"Oh, I shoplift, too," said Timothy Senior. "It's the only way to survive between work contracts." Such was the way of life here. The next day, I was gifted a huge wad of Parmesan cheese, delivered to me by one of my new friends, compliments of Loblaws (so they said).

That weekend on the beach, I related the story of my fellow residents, the shoplifting artists, to a friend who had ferried out from the city to spend the afternoon with me and to visit the residency one last time before it was seized by the bank. My friend, who was also an artist, nodded along as I told him about Loblaws and the 30 percent skim.

"Oh, yes, I do that, too," he said. "If it's a big chain and I'm broke, I just take what I need." This was how artists survived in Toronto.

If I lived in Toronto, would I, too, have to become a professional shoplifter?

I knew that this probably wouldn't be possible. I was personally always too fearful to shoplift even a handful of chocolate-coated almonds from the bulk bin at the grocery store chain in the mountain town where I grew up. I'd stand in front of the bins but was physically unable to move my limbs to reach in. Instead, I got my friends to pilfer the candy for me. As I did again, years later, with the Parmesan cheese.

As I write this, the heel of Parmesan cheese sits in my fridge, and every time I grate it over a salad or a dish of pasta, I think of the island, the beach beside Ontario's inland sea, the blissful days that seemed to stretch the length of the shore, moving between manuscript, notebook, daydream, and cold plunge.

2

On the last day of the residency, a group of us roasted marshmallows around the fire. There was a sense of sadness in the air; most of us would be going back to our homes and our jobs, our uncreative lives. The conversation turned, as it often does in these situations, to worst jobs. When my turn came, I told them about my most recent one, which had essentially been to teach language skills to the CEOs of tomorrow at a local business school.

The course was designed to give young venture capitalists a sense of ethical responsibility about their place in the world.

The idea was that if they were going to be upper-level cogs in the machine, they should at least be conscious of their cog status. A self-aware cog that still goes about its business but can think critically about false equivalencies, straw men, and slippery slopes.

My students' first assignment in this class was to write a complaint letter to a business and demand retribution for poor customer service or a disappointing product. One student wrote to management at Louis Vuitton to complain that a zipper in an inner pocket of her $2,500 handbag had ceased to function. She'd only used the bag twice in the nine months since purchasing. How will you make this better? she asked Louis Vuitton, as if expecting a personal response from the nineteenth-century trunk maker. *How will you make this up to me?* This was what the university had taught her to do: advocate for herself against the injustices of the world. It wasn't her fault that she'd never experienced any.

Other students told me woefully that they couldn't think of anything to complain about. They had no complaints — that was their complaint. One unoriginally suggested he'd write a letter to the course coordinator complaining about the assignment. "Go ahead," I said, still thinking, *How did one spend $2,500 on a handbag?* I imagined their pillared family homes in Oakville, Westmount, or New Jersey while assessing their complaint letters and thought about how nothing could touch their realm, not inflation or low grades, not even the environmental crisis. Their parents probably had access to elite underground bunkers in the Black Hills of South Dakota, or those gated communities carved into the mountains of Switzerland or into the South African desert, wherein everyone wore Louis Vuitton handbags twice before discarding them for an invisible imperfection. I imagined my heart to be an inner zipper, the innermost in my body, that was now a little more broken after reading the students' complaint letters.

I held office hours in a communal adjunct lecturers' office that was crowded with chairs and tables in various states of disrepair and often smelled vaguely of moist processed meat sandwiches. Five adjuncts shared the room, though I only ever saw two others: both engineering professors who split their day between three different institutions. It was in this office on Wednesdays when I regularly met with a stream of students who arrived to complain about the grades received for their complaint letters.

One of those students, Anthony, wore suits to class and treated me with the wry, smiling casualness of a colleague rather than his instructor. One Wednesday, after negotiating a C+ up to a B, Anthony told me his life plan. I wasn't sure why he decided to disclose his ambitions to me — perhaps because he knew I was a writer, which I learned was something he planned to be once he made his fortune in investment banking. He'd retire at forty, he explained, leaning back in his chair. It was still a lifetime away for him, but it was good to think ahead. Anthony planned to buy a large house in the south of France that he'd fill with "art."

"What kind of art?" I asked.

He seemed surprised at this question. "Famous art," he clarified. He told me he read Jung and Nietzsche at night because he wasn't just an ordinary business major but someone who valued the life of the mind as well as the life of the pocket.

At one point during our meeting, he asked me about my own work. I'd recently published a poetry chapbook, so I spoke about the process of putting the collection together. He leaned forward in his seat and confessed that he, too, aspired to write poetry. I asked him if he'd written anything yet, and he admitted he hadn't. He knew he was capable of great ideas; they just hadn't been formulated on the page yet. He asked me what the trick was to knowing which words to use and when to use them. For a moment, the knowing look dropped from his eyes and he seemed a little embarrassed. He asked, "How do I learn to think like you?"

It was curious to me that this young man was interested in the creative life. What value did it hold for those who had money, or were about to make a lot of it? They could just hire someone to do the difficult labour of art. To ghost-live the disappointment, exhilaration, perseverance, and rejection for them.

I wanted to tell him: Go off and live a happy, unexamined life. Call me up in twenty years' time and appoint me as permanent writer-in-residence in your French villa. But his request appeared to be earnest, so instead I told him to read. Read a lot. To which he replied that he didn't have time. Straightening his tie, he said, "When I buy my house in France, I'll have all the time in the world. I'll be old, but I'll have all the time. I'll become a whole new person."

• • •

"To become a whole new person," Timothy Senior mused. "To become whole and new. How does one do that?"

"I don't think it's possible," said Boris. "Once a capitalist, always a capitalist."

Camille disagreed. "I think people can change," she said. "But CEO to poet — that would be a big shift."

I told the group that should my former student ever invite me to be writer-in-residence in his villa in the south of France, I'd bring them all with me.

• • •

"How do I learn to think like you?" I often think about Anthony's question. It wasn't a simple one to answer. But if I were to try in earnest, these would be my instructions:

> Carry a notebook and record the most mundane things in the most unusual sentences. Ride a hot air balloon along the earth's melting surface. Watch its fires from a distance, the red sooty legions of industry crawling Arcticward like stretch marks. Crochet your way out of sadness using undyed wool. Rediscover yourself in someone else's handwriting on a birthday card. Fill your windows with minute replicas from that lost garden in the Pacific, that first garden where the pothos vine is also known as devil's ivy. Flaunt your depressive realism; the future comes from inside you. Discharge your politics in non-rhyming couplets. Speak in the calm tones of a freshly ironed shirt. Know the difference between nature poetry and environmental poetry. Take the heart's first exit. Search public opinion for details about the drug that changes your life by making food repulsive. Imagine being hungry and repulsed, steadily chewing a dark vegetable from the top to the root. Adore on a cellular level the writing of Marguerite Duras. Categorize your insecurity by Netflix genre. Forgive the friends who found happiness and

didn't invite you into it. Dust the ficus so she can breathe through her webbed green face. Listen to the mute wisdom of the street lamp. Stop and bend to tie your right shoe and then your left. Pit your SSRIs against each other. Share your sandwiches with the adjuncts. No longer be a remorseful buyer of jumpsuits. Give in to solitude, this vast inner solitude that has already flooded the grasses of Saskatchewan. In the blood thrum of indecision, make your bed. Bathe. Stroke Louis Vuitton's luxurious moustache. No longer be beholden to the life of the pocket. Rinse hands twice. Rub vitamin E into your own stretch marks. Ignore email alerts. Float two feet above the flood. Give your body up for kite material. You'll make a beautiful kite. Build your life around your necessity for air. Dream in your kited dreams about the atmospheric river over California, about glassy Christmas lakes, a white angora coat with its seams intact. Dream of new verbs, of new conjugations. Step off the bus and let winter slush its epiphany at your feet.

3

Upon returning home to Montreal from the island, I was invited to a poetry reading at what appeared to be the outskirts of the observable universe. It was a garden in a northern neighbourhood in Montreal, past Autoroute 40, where a group of artists were growing plants to use as fabric dyes. The familiar streets and parks fell away as my friend Brennan and I cycled along the commuter rail track and hauled our bikes across the overpass, below us traffic streaming orange in the sunset. We wound past Canadian Tire and Costco, through the tall industrial buildings of the former garment district. We finally pulled over at the entrance to a construction zone. On one side of the zone roared a four-lane highway. On the other, several pieces of enormous construction equipment gleamed in the light, abandoned for the evening. My phone claimed we'd arrived.

"Do you think we have the wrong address?" I asked Brennan before noticing a little farther down the path, twisted in the branches of a clump of dark trees, a glimmer of fairy lights.

There were other bikes strewn alongside the path, slim-framed with seventies-style handlebars, half hidden in the waist-length grass. I noticed a beer crate beside a small shed, and then up ahead, in a loose circle around a makeshift stage, a crowd of people listening intently. On the stage stood a young woman in a pale linen dress and long brown hair reading poetry off her phone as the commuter train rumbled past, and almost simultaneously, a plane ripped over us en route to the airport. From where I stood, the poet was completely inaudible.

I handed Brennan a beer and found a seat at a picnic table, which held scones, a bowl of whipping cream, and a pay-what-you-can box.

As I sat down, I was reminded of another night, years before, and winding through a neighbourhood that was also considered industrial at the time in search of a secret cinema. A white metal door opened in a white wall, like a sudden interruption of reality. I shook the snow off my coat and entered. On the far wall a black-and-white film erupted into movement. I'd come alone — how often I went out alone in those days — drawn by a loose invitation, the promise of a plot. I don't remember the film, just a wash of dark and light on the wall and a beer in my hand, maybe a conversation with a stranger, also leaning against the wall. The details are no longer available to me, just the memory of being lost and then the wall suddenly opening like a pocket in an advent calendar to reveal a dark world alive with people.

This was something of the same experience except it was summer and I rarely went places alone anymore. In fact, it was hard to picture that younger, independent, more stubborn, more hopeful version of myself.

Over the course of the next few hours, the poets, all beautiful and elfin — many of them in their twenties — got up on the stage, with its tiny lights and gauzy frame curtains, and read from their recent work. All were working on new writing daily, and they seemed to be filled with discipline and commitment. Some of their words were lost to the traffic, the commuter rail, and the flight path overhead, but as the sun went down on the garden, I began to hear their voices more clearly. I heard a voice I recognized and saw that my friend S had stood up to read. The poems were ones I recognized, chameleon ones that had changed since I'd last read them, printed out for our writing circle, but they retained something so singular — like a signature or a hand-drawn map.

Stars appeared in the sky, the heat of the July day seemed to evaporate with the traffic, and in that moment, I understood what drew the poets to this garden lodged between thoroughfare and industry with its diesel-flavoured wind and low-flying planes. This garden was one of the last undesirable plots of land in the city. That was surely what made it so valuable: that it was commercially useless, and so could be filled with commercially useless things, like poetry and plant life.

After the reading concluded, S joined me for a glass of wine at the picnic table. She sat across from me, checks flushed and hair lit up by the twinkling stage lights. She wanted to hear about Gibraltar Point.

I told her how my weeks on the island had been some of the happiest of my year, and how later, on the train back to Montreal, I questioned why that was the case. Was this simply because of my morning ritual in the water and the dedicated time and space to write without guilt? Was it because of the multi-generational and communal meals, the free time, or the s'mores and midnight skinny-dipping? Was it because I'd made some fast friends and was reminded that it was still possible to make friends in one's late thirties? Summer camp for artists, Boris had called the island retreat. Here there was no good reason why, in Georgia O'Keeffe's words, we shouldn't "live always."

It was all these things, but it was something more urgent as well.

Living at the residency during its collapse had prompted larger, fundamental questions about the state of the arts in Canada. What is a city without its artists? What is a country without its artists? In a moment in history when artists and creative spaces are under threat, how and where does art survive? Being part of the defiant, collective spirit, I realized, had made me feel energized rather than wracked with despair. I was reminded that artists are resilient and resourceful. We'll find a way to stay, even if it means unofficially taxing the Loblaws produce aisle.

• • •

As my train home sped east through Prince Edward County, I wondered, Was I unhappy? Was this the name I'd give to the shapeless permanent feeling that stunts creativity and invites self-doubt? How could I bring the artist residency into my everyday life?

I wasn't alone in asking this question. The answer seemed to always come back to space: the room, the studio, the salon, the garden on the edge of the city. It came back to protecting that space.

Feminist scholars, urban reformers, and architects have been grappling with the question of space and creativity for well over a century. Socializing housework, they argued, turning domestic work into salaried labour instead of invisible feminized and individualized labour, was key to allowing women more time to work, study, and create art. They also advocated for a semi-communal setup where food could be prepared and shared in common spaces, reducing isolation.

The artist residency bore surprising similarities to some of these proposed feminist housing projects and other models of community living that gained brief popularity at the turn of the twentieth century before they were eventually replaced by the detached single-family home model. For instance, the American writer and nineteenth-century feminist Charlotte Perkins Gilman — author of the short story "The Yellow Wallpaper" — advocated for what she called the "feminist apartment hotel," a semi-communal boarding house attuned to the needs of working mothers. Composed of kitchenless private units, the apartment hotels had shared centralized cooking and dining facilities, roof gardens, and professional nurses and teachers taking care of the residents' children in a nursery or kindergarten within the building. Earlier in the summer, Artscape had hosted a group residency for artist mothers that operated very much like Gilman's feminist apartment hotel.

I mentioned the feminist hotel to S, since she was working on a project that tracked changing city spaces and had been conducting interviews with artists in Montreal.

"Maybe we can resurrect it," she suggested.

We'd already plotted out what our poets' commune would look like. A wild field beside a lake, but close enough to the city so we could travel in to see art. We'd only work occasionally when we needed cash. Everyone would have a room of their own. Now we just needed to convince our friends to quit their jobs and join us.

The early-twentieth-century designer and social reformer Alice Constance Austin had even more radical plans than ours. Rather than just a hotel or a commune, she planned to build a socialist city. Llano Del Rio would be a circular city of ten thousand people inscribed within one square mile of land. Each kitchenless house was to be connected to a central kitchen, staffed by professionals, through a complex underground network of tunnels and railway cars. These underground railways would bring cooked food and fresh laundry to shared hubs, from which small electric cars would dispatch the deliveries to the basement of each house. Once the food was consumed and the linen used, the food containers and laundry would be returned to the central facilities for washing in an industrial machine helmed by paid workers, both women and men. Austin believed:

> The Socialist City should be beautiful … illustrating in a concrete way the solidarity of the community; it should emphasize the fundamental principle of equal opportunity for all; and it should be the last word in the application of scientific discovery to everyday

> life, putting every labor saving device at the service of every citizen.[4]

"Did the city ever get built?" S asked.

"Partly. The colony existed for a time in Antelope Valley in northern Los Angeles County," I told her. "Then they ran out of water. The underground network never existed, though."

"Too bad," said S. "I'd love an underground railway laundry system."

We added this feature to our commune bucket list.

Austin's idea that the aesthetics of a city illustrate in a concrete way the equality of its community reminded S of a similar argument made by the urban historian Jane Jacobs in *The Death and Life of Great American Cities*. Jacobs believed that cities provide "something for everybody, only because, and only when, they are created by everybody."[5] (I recently learned that this quote is also inscribed on the northeast side of Davenport Road and Christie Street in Toronto.) When cities fail, they fail for the same reasons democracies fail: corruption, tyranny, homogenization, overspecialization, cultural drift, and atrophy.

"This city is definitely failing us," I said as we gazed across the poet's garden to the giant crane looming in the adjacent lot. Then it occurred to me that all the cities I'd lived in were failing cities. At the same time, there was nowhere else to go.

"Maybe I'll go back to the island permanently," I suggested. "Live on wild kale, surrounded by other artists, writing, painting, or building our driftwood monuments on the beach."

"And in the winter?" asked S.

"We'll build a fire."

I told S about how when the residency staff were suddenly laid off we shared the chores and kept order. How the dishes were always clean and stacked to dry. How we kept all hours, some rising at dawn, some painting till 3:00 a.m. How we sat outside in the evening around shared plates of food until the bugs started eating us alive.

"Perhaps the artist residency is the blueprint for our artist city," I said. "We just need to build it. Or are we too tired to build it?"

S said she'd read an article that day that forecast an imminent revolution. Earlier that week, she'd performed at another event, a poetry reading in an old warehouse building in the south of the city. Most of the readers had been in their early twenties then as well.

"The younger generation is angry," S said now, swirling her wine. "Angrier than us."

Above her, a plane swung low across the sky toward the airport. A train pulled into the commuter rail station, pausing before snaking north over the river.

"The revolution is coming," S said. "Within the next five years or so. I wonder what it will look like."

Postscript

Freedom isn't enough. What I desire doesn't have a name yet.
— Clarice Lispector, *Near to the Wild Heart*

NOT LONG AFTER THE POETRY READING IN THE GARDEN between the highway and commuter train, I uprooted my life once more, this time for my first permanent academic position. My partner and I drove east with our two tarsier-eyed cats (now adopted) in an overstuffed car to the Maritimes. As I unlocked the door to my new office, I realized this was the first time I truly had a room of my own. It was a strange thing to think and write about this space for so many years and then to arrive here at a designated desk, a window bright with the late-summer sun, an empty bookcase, and a door with my name on it.

Was this how Leslie Marmon Silko felt in her unrented law office? Or Maya Angelou in her empty hotel room? What would I write in this room? What rituals would I cultivate here?

Now that I had the space and relative security, a new (old) challenge announced itself: time.

As I unpacked my books and organized them in the wall of built-in shelves, I came across my old weather-beaten copy of *A Room of One's Own*. It was the same dog-eared one that my friend had delivered to me in Montreal and that I now carried with me like a passport. We'd been travelling together for many years through many different rooms.

Before she died, Virginia Woolf was working on what she conceived of as a sequel to *A Room of One's Own*. In a version of this essay, delivered as a lecture to a branch of the National Society for Women's Service, she again mentioned the habit of freedom. "You have won rooms of your own in the houses hitherto exclusively owned by men," she commended her listeners. "But this freedom is only a beginning."[1]

This is a good reminder: that there was and is still much ground to cover. That the process of cultivating and defending one's freedom is active and ongoing.

"The room is your own, but it is still bare," Woolf continued. "It has to be furnished; it has to be decorated; it has to be shared. How are you going to furnish it, how are you going to decorate it? With whom are you going to share it, and upon what terms?"[2]

I've been thinking a lot about these questions as I furnish and decorate my own room, as I decide what authors, artists, and books I want to invite into this space. Over the course of my journey to this room, I've become better at defining my terms — the conditions for my writing practice. I've grown more skilled at defending my time. I've become more comfortable with solitude, more comfortable living, like Joni Mitchell's artist, inside a box of paints, but also taking breaks from that box sometimes.

But there are still days in which I second-guess myself, succumb to self-doubt, or the mousetrap of perfectionism. Even with a room, even in a creative profession, there are days when I'm levelled by the uncreative life, by the crises on the newsreel, or by a melancholy more detailed than the world. On these days, when I feel as if I'm starting again at zero, furnishing my room from scratch, I remind myself to pick up a book, hold it up to my face to listen to the collective hum of creative companionship — all those thinkers and artists who managed to keep making and doing and being.

This book, too, has been an effort to summon that creative companionship. It's been a way to invite readers into my room, not the one I'm currently sitting in, but the room my imagination sits in, with its domed glass roof, sailing across space and time.

What I've learned in my journey through these pages is that making space for women among monuments, making space for all individuals striving to live a creative life, is a collaborative undertaking. It can't be accomplished alone. Perhaps, together, we'll resurrect the feminist city with its underground laundry railway system. We'll proliferate the artist colony with its communal gardens of sunflowers and wild kale. Or at least we might strive to live by the ideals and practices these spaces allow. To defend, every day, our right to creative community and free time: to live in rooms both lonely and marvellous. To remember that this freedom is only a beginning and that possibly this freedom isn't enough. That what we desire might not even have a name yet.

Acknowledgements

THANK YOU TO MY EDITOR, MEGHAN MACDONALD, FOR THE warmth, encouragement, and discerning edits. Much gratitude to everyone at Dundurn Press who helped bring this book into the world. A special thank-you to Laura Boyle for the beautiful cover. Thank you to Michael Carroll for the great copy-edits and to Janna Green and Amber McMillan for the editorial support. Another big thank-you to T. Liem and Catriona Wright for generously reading chapter drafts.

I am grateful to the Fonds de recherche du Québec, the Canada Council for the Arts, the Banff Centre for Arts and Creativity, and Arts New Brunswick for supporting the writing of this book and for the Busteed fund for supplementing the editorial process. "Under Agatha Christie" appeared under the title "A Writer in Eight Landscapes" on Rob McClennan's blog, *My (Small-Press) Writing Day.* Excerpts from the book have also appeared in *Maisonneuve Magazine* and *Geist.* Many thanks to the editors. An early version of "Books We Sleep With" was published under the title "Why I Left Men for Books" in *Electric Literature*. My appreciation to the editors there, and to all the readers who reached out to me to let me know they felt heard.

To recall Alice Walker's words: "A writer, to be connected to the world, should have a circle that cares about the world. And out of that would come the writing." I thank this wide circle of friends and family in my own life, you who have made writing possible for me.

Thank you especially to my trusted writing group and its different iterations over the years. Even if we're no longer in the same city, I am forever grateful for your years of support. A big thank-you to all the readers who participated in the collage for "Books we sleep with": Eliza, Emmanuelle, Paige, Sunita, T, Sarah, Annie, Dzitka, and Mateo. Thank you to Eliza Robertson for thinking through ideas of female solitude with me in the early stages of the book. Thank you to Myra Bloom for the conversations on life writing and feminist refusal and for being a wonderful collaborator. Appreciation to those who invited me to share my research for this book: Carlos A. Pittella and Jason Camlot for inviting me to read at Concordia University's Creatique, and to the English departments at McGill and Dalhousie Universities for inviting me to give talks on the book-in-progress. So much gratitude to Holly Vestad for the fine editorial eye and for cheering me on to the finish line.

Finally, thank you to Greg for being there for me and for reminding me not to stay up too late. Thank you to my family for supporting my "odd" choices, most significantly, my attempt to live a creative life.

To my mom and my sisters, this book is for you.

Notes

Preface: First Woman Ph.D.

1 King James Bible, 1 Timothy 2:12.

2 There's one easy-to-miss exception in this gallery of men — a bust of the sixteenth-century poet Gaspara Stampa, considered one of the greatest female poets of the Renaissance. Her bust is relegated to a spot at the feet of a male statue, the sculptor Andrea Briosco. Stampa is about the size of a suitcase, the kind that fits into the overhead bin on an Air Canada plane.

3 Federica Arcoraci quoted in Angela Giuffrida, "Italy: Proposal for Statue of First Woman to Get PhD Sparks Debate," *The Guardian*, January 3, 2022, theguardian.com/world/2022/jan/03/italy-proposal-statue-elena-cornaro-piscopia-first-woman-phd-debate.

4 Angela Giuffrida, "Padua Plans First Female Statue — But Probably Not with the 78 Male Ones in the Main Square," *The Guardian*, February 2, 2022, theguardian.com/world/2022/feb/02/padua-plans-first-female-statue-but-78-men-may-keep-main-square#:~:text=In%20order%20to%20overcome%20the,be%20one%20of%20a%20woman.

5 Virginia Woolf, *A Room of One's Own*, 113.

6 Leonora Carrington, *Down Below* (*The New York Review of Books*, 2017), 19.

7 The stories in this book are true, yet as this is a work of creative non-fiction, the conversations and events are portrayed to the best of my memory. I've also occasionally compressed events or folded two conversations into one for literary effect. Some names and identifying details have been changed to protect the privacy of the people involved.

8 I understand the term *woman* to include non-cisgendered women and women who identify as trans or nonbinary. I believe that a definition of the term that fails to respect trans identities is incompatible with feminism's commitment to eradicating women's oppression.

2 Next Picasso

1 For an example, see Michelangelo's *Night*, a reclining figure with breasts that look like two scoops of hard ice cream blobbed onto a boy's torso as an afterthought.

2 Vivek Shraya writes: "What would my body look and feel like if I didn't have to mould it into both a shield and an ornament?" See Vivek Shraya, *I'm Afraid of Men* (Penguin Canada, 2018), 31.

3 Later, I read the film critic Laura Mulvey's treatise on how the "male gaze projects its fantasy onto the female figure, which is styled accordingly" and started to really question how I was implicated in this way of seeing. See Laura Mulvey, "Visual Pleasure and Narrative Cinema," *Screen* 16, no. 3 (Autumn 1975): 6–18.

4 Jamaica Kincaid, *Lucy* (Farrar, Straus and Giroux, 1990), 95.

5 In his analysis of the masculine gaze in visual art, John Berger sums up the history of Western art succinctly: "*Men act* and *women appear*." John Berger, *Ways of Seeing* (British Broadcasting Corporation and Penguin Books, 1972), 47. But by claiming the role of photographer, Lucy refuses to "appear." She is the observer behind the lens — the one to assess the quality of the light, select the f-stop, the aperture, then to frame, capture, and create the image.

6 It's in her encounter with Gauguin's paintings, her confrontation with the watcher/watched or artist/muse dichotomy, that Lucy identifies the enormous disparity between herself and the painter: "I was not a man; I was a young woman from the fringes of the world, and when I left my home I had wrapped around my shoulders the mantle of a servant" (Kincaid, *Lucy*, 95). There comes a time in every girl's life when she realizes that, paradoxically, she is unable to be both a person and a woman. This is what Kincaid captures so well in Lucy, yet, of course, as a young woman of colour from the West Indies in 1960s America, Lucy is quadruply marginalized by gender, race, class, and her status as migrant from an island with a violent history of colonization and slavery.

7 As Audre Lorde has written, "Anger is loaded with information and energy ... I have tried to learn my anger's usefulness to me, as well as its limitations." See "The Uses of Anger: Women Responding to Racism," in *Sister Outsider: Essays and Speeches* (Crossing Press, 1984), 127–31.

8 Virginia Woolf, "Professions for Women," in *The Norton Anthology of Literature by Women: The Tradition in English*, 3rd ed., vol. 2 (W.W. Norton, 2007), 244.

9 I'm reminded of a line from social critic bell hooks on the subject of autobiography. By writing about memory and through memory, hooks reflected that she "wanted not to forget the past but to break its hold." See bell hooks, "Writing Autobiography," in *Talking Back: Thinking Feminist, Thinking Black* (Routledge, 2015), 261. This seems to be Kincaid's project as well: not to forget the past but to break its hold. In fact, Kincaid changed her name from Elaine Potter Richardson to Jamaica Kincaid in 1973 when her writing was first published, describing this name change as a way "to do things without being the same person who couldn't do them — the same person who had all these weights" (quoted in Leslie Garis, *The New York Times*, October 7, 1990). In the novel, Lucy's

full name is Lucy Josephine Potter, an echo of Kincaid's former name. Writing the novel, it appears, was another way of casting off some of those unwanted weights.

10 It hadn't occurred to me that writing and raising a child are both gruelling and creative ambitions. I hadn't yet read Bernadette Mayer, a poet who turned the experience of motherhood and the constraints of domestic life into poetry. In my experience, reproductive care and artmaking had always existed in opposition to each other. I was only just beginning to question why this was the case — in other words, to question the so-called natural order of things.

3 Art Monsters in Paris

1 The name of the ekphrastic poem by Rainer Maria Rilke that ends with his famous line, "You must change your life," is "Archaic Torso of Apollo."

2 As Lauren Elkin shows us in her recent book, *Art Monsters: Unruly Bodies in Feminist Art* (Farrar, Straus and Giroux, 2023), inspired by this term, the expression "art monster" exists in French: *Monstre de l'art* refers to "someone big and important and unreasonable. Male, obviously. Charismatic, an egomaniac" (5).

3 Jenny Offill, *Dept. of Speculation* (Alfred A. Knopf, 2014), 8.

4 Rachel Cusk, "Can a Woman Who Is an Artist Ever Just Be an Artist?" *New York Times Magazine*, November 7, 2019, nytimes.com/2019/11/07/magazine/women-art-celia-paul-cecily-brown.html.

5 Woolf, *A Room of One's Own*, 49.

6 Toni Morrison, *Sula* (Vintage, 2004), 121.

7 This unhappy love triangle was the subject of Gertrude Stein's *Q.E.D.* and "Melanctha," written in the decade after leaving Baltimore.

8 Woody Allen was accused of sexually assaulting his adopted daughter Dylan Farrow in 1992, when she was seven years old. Two investigations subsequently cleared him, but Dylan reiterated the charge in 2014, supported by her brother Ronan Farrow.

9 Gertrude Stein, *The Autobiography of Alice B. Toklas* (Penguin, 2020), 60.

10 Stein, *The Autobiography of Alice B. Toklas*, 35.

11 Stein, *The Autobiography of Alice B. Toklas*, 19.

12 Quoted in Janet Malcolm, "Gertrude Stein's War," *The New Yorker*, May 25, 2003, newyorker.com/magazine/2003/06/02/gertrude-steins-war.

13 Bernadette Mayer, *Midwinter Day* (New Directions, 1999), 32.

14 Quoted in Stein, *The Autobiography of Alice B. Toklas*, 56.

15 Michael Prodger, "The Picasso Problem," *The New Statesman*, July 26, 2023, newstatesman.com/culture/art-design/2023/07/picasso-50th-anniversary.

16 Miles J. Unger writes of this portrait of Raymonde and her return to the orphanage in his biography of Picasso: "There's no indication that Picasso ever abused Raymonde, but it's clear she aroused feelings in him that might have led to disaster. His attraction to adolescent girls, at least later in life, is well-documented." See Miles J. Unger, *Picasso and the Painting That Shocked the World* (Simon & Schuster, 2018), 314.

17 Saidiya Hartman, "An Unnamed Girl, a Speculative Fiction," *The New Yorker*, February 9, 2019, newyorker.com/culture/culture-desk/an-unnamed-girl-a-speculative-history. After the publication of Hartman's essay on the unnamed girl, the image was scrubbed from the Web and classified as child pornography. Now only a cropped version of the photograph is shown in Hartman's article.

4 Almost Genius

1 In England, sepsis, due to the casual use of non-sterile techniques, remained the cause of half of the total maternal deaths until the early 1940s when penicillin began to be used outside the lab.

2 Charlotte Brontë's physician ascribed her death to tuberculosis, but later evaluation of her symptoms has led experts to conclude

that the cause of her death was hyperemesis gravidarum, a pregnancy complication that at the time was ascribed to neurosis: the mother's rejection of her pregnancy and her femininity. Her doctor may have believed he was performing an act of service: better to die of blameless tuberculosis than to have brought death upon herself because of her ideas of female independence.

3 Maggie Nelson, *The Argonauts* (Graywolf Press, 2015), 57–58.

4 See Alice Walker, *In Search of Our Mothers' Gardens: Womanist Prose* (Harcourt, 2004). The term *Motheroot,* as Walker says, was inspired by Marilou Awiakta's poem "Motheroot."

5 Mayer, *Midwinter Day,* 53.

6 Some of Kate Chopin's critics dismissed the novel as "sex fiction" (*Chicago Times-Herald*) and "poison" (*St. Louis Republic*), lamenting her fate of becoming "one more clever writer gone wrong" (*The Nation*). Even the writer Willa Cather called the novel "trite and sordid" (*Pittsburgh Leader*).

7 Kate Chopin, *The Awakening* (Herbert S. Stone, 1899), 71.

8 Chopin, *The Awakening,* 122.

9 Due to poor sales, her publisher cancelled the publication of her third story collection, *A Vocation and a Voice. The Awakening* fell out of print for more than fifty years until its themes found relevance in the 1970s with the rise of the second-wave feminist movement.

10 Fred Lewis Pattee, *A History of American Literature Since 1870* (The Century Company, 1915), 364.

11 Christine Battersby, *Gender and Genius: Towards a Feminist Aesthetics* (Indiana University Press, 1989), 28.

12 Battersby, *Gender and Genius,* 33.

13 One interesting thing to note is that a distinction was made between the terms *woman* and *feminine*: "One thing the history of the concept of 'genius' reveals is that being a woman and being 'feminine' are radically different things. It is *women* who have been excluded from culture, not the 'feminine.'" See Battersby, *Gender and Genius,* 138. As Romanticism gained

influence in the nineteenth century, bringing about changes in aesthetic values, the feminine was appropriated and even valued as the very qualities that distinguished the ordinary man from the extraordinary man or genius. Instead of satire and wit, the prized aesthetics of the geniuses of the Age of Reason, the Romantic period favoured in the male poet traits traditionally associated with femininity, such as being intuitive and receptive, being emotional and in touch with nature's rhythms, even having the capacity to "give birth" to artistic creations. John Keats and Percy Bysshe Shelley are good examples of this. The creative woman, however, remained the pseudo-male, a freak whose intellectual and artistic ingenuity went against the nature of her procreativity. What seemed natural in the male poet was monstrous in the female poet.

14 Quoted in Todd Goddard, "Scribbling Women," omeka.uvu.edu/exhibits/show/scribblingwomen/menu.

15 Emily Dickinson, *The Poems of Emily Dickinson: Reading Edition*, ed. Ralph W. Franklin (Harvard University Press, 1999), 206.

16 Linda Nochlin, "Why Have There Been No Great Women Artists?," *ARTnews*, May 30, 2015, artnews.com/art-news/retrospective/why-have-there-been-no-great-women-artists-4201.

17 Simone de Beauvoir, *The Second Sex*, ed. and trans. H.M. Parshley (Vintage Books, 1989).

18 Megan Garber, "David Foster Wallace and the Dangerous Romance of Male Genius," *The Atlantic*, May 9, 2018, theatlantic.com/entertainment/archive/2018/05/the-world-still-spins-around-male-genius/559925.

19 Julia Kristeva, "Is There a Feminine Genius?," *Critical Inquiry* 30, no. 3 (Spring 2004): 493.

20 Following on from Virginia Woolf, Alice Walker outlines the life of the enslaved writer Phillis Wheatley, whose genius was more marginalized and thwarted than that of the imagined

Judith Shakespeare. "What then are we to make of Phillis Wheatley, a slave, who owned not even herself?" writes Walker. "This sickly, frail black girl who required a servant of her own at times — her health was so precarious and who, had she been white, would have been easily considered the intellectual superior of all the women and most of the men in the society of her day." See Walker, *In Search of Our Mothers' Gardens*, 235.

21 Woolf, *A Room of One's Own*, 48, 113.

22 Leonora Carrington, *The Complete Stories of Leonora Carrington* (Dorothy Project, 2017). The quote "Angels must be devoured" is from Carrington's short story "A Mexican Fairy Tale."

5 Allegorical Women

1 Angela Carter, *Nights at the Circus* (Penguin, 1986).

2 Angela Carter, "Notes from the Front Line," in *On Gender and Writing*, ed. Micheline Wandor (Pandora, 1983), 69.

3 Carter, *Nights at the Circus*, 25. I'm also reminded of the advice from the performance artist Kate Bornstein: "Become a more frightening monster than the one they think you are" (*Hello, Cruel World: 101 Alternatives to Suicide for Teens, Freaks, and Other Outlaws* [Seven Stories Press, 2006]).

4 Marina Warner, *Monuments & Maidens: The Allegory of the Female Form* (Atheneum, 1985), xix–xx.

5 Woolf, *A Room of One's Own*, 56.

6 Angus Fletcher, *Allegory: The Theory of a Symbolic Mode* (Cornell University Press, 1964), 23.

7 In many cases, the existing monuments represent problematic historic figures who don't merit public honouring. There have been recent global movements to tear down the monuments of such figures — like the slave owner James McGill in Montreal, for example, or the Cecil Rhodes Memorial in Cape Town.

8 Details and quotations about the case are taken from Sean O'Hagan, "Ana Mendieta: The Death of an Artist Foretold in Blood," *The*

Guardian, September 22, 2013, theguardian.com/artanddesign/2013/sep/22/ana-mendieta-artist-work-foretold-death.

9 The statue's hollowness, Marina Warner points out, is "a prerequisite of symbols with infinite powers of endurance and adaptability ... she is given meaning by us, and it can change according to what we see and want." See Warner, *Monuments & Maidens*, 11.

10 Warner, *Monuments & Maidens*, 11–12.

6 The Uncreative Life

1 Quoted in Elissa Schappell and Claudia Brodsky Lacour, "Toni Morrison, the Art of Fiction, No. 134," *The Paris Review* 128 (Fall 1993), theparisreview.org/interviews/1888/the-art-of-fiction-no-134-toni-morrison.

2 Quoted in Adam Fitzgerald, "Lives of the Poets: Bernadette Mayer," *Poetry Foundation*, April 4, 2011, poetryfoundation.org/articles/69658/lives-of-the-poets-bernadette-mayer.

3 N. Scott Momaday, "Spirit of the Woods," *The New York Times*, May 24, 1981, nytimes.com/1981/05/24/books/the-spirit-in-words.html.

4 Leslie Marmon Silko, *Ceremony* (Penguin Books, 1977), xii.

5 See ketchikanstories.com/ketchicon/chief-johnsons-totem-pole/totem-pole?slide=7.

6 Silko, *Ceremony*, xiii.

7 Silko, *Ceremony*, xiii.

8 Quoted in Kenneth M. Pierce, "Education: The Most Happy Fellows," *Time*, August 8, 1983, time.com/archive/6700877/education-the-most-happy-fellows.

9 Schappell and Lacour, "Toni Morrison, the Art of Fiction."

10 In 1924, the year they got married, Jo Nivison recommended Edward Hopper's work to the curators of a group show she'd exhibited in, and as a result of the exposure she'd secured for him, Hopper was given a sellout solo show by the gallery that represented him for the rest of his life. See Gaby Wood, "Man

and Muse," *The Observer*, April 25, 2004, theguardian.com /artanddesign/2004/apr/25/art1.

11 Yet her waning art practice wasn't just a result of her dedication to supporting her husband's art. As Olivia Laing explains in her art biography and treatise on loneliness, *The Lonely City*, Hopper "didn't just fail to support Jo's painting, but rather worked actively to discourage it, mocking and denigrating the few things she did manage to produce, and acting with great creativity and malice to limit the conditions in which she might paint." See Olivia Laing, *The Lonely City: Adventures in the Art of Being Alone* (Picador, 2016), 37.

12 Quoted in Sarah McColl, "Jo Hopper, Woman in the Sun," *The Paris Review*, February 26, 2018, theparisreview.org /blog/2018/02/26/jo-hopper-woman-sun-woman-shadow.

13 Octavia E. Butler, "Furor Scribendi," *Bloodchild and Other Stories* (Seven Stories Press, 2005), 141.

14 Alice Munro, *Munro's Best: Selected Stories* (McClelland & Stewart, 2006), x.

15 Alice Munro, "Writing's Something I Did Like the Ironing," *The Globe and Mail*, December 11, 1982: E1.

16 Gail Scott, *Spaces Like Stairs: Essays* (Women's Press, 1989), 187.

17 Tillie Olsen, *Silences* (Delacorte Press/Seymour Lawrence, 1978), 33.

18 Olsen, *Silences*, 18–19.

19 Walker, *In Search of Our Mothers' Gardens*, 238–40.

20 Alice Munro, "The Office," in *Dance of the Happy Shades* (McGraw-Hill Ryerson, 1968), 59–60.

21 Interview between Maya Angelou and Claudia Tate, quoted in Mason Currey, *Daily Rituals: How Artists Work* (Alfred A. Knopf, 2013), 122.

22 Henri Lefebvre, *Everyday Life in the Modern World* (Transaction Books, 1971), 73.

23 De Beauvoir, *The Second Sex*, 722.

24 De Certeau differentiates between "strategies" and "tactics" to explain this power struggle. A strategy is the overarching

framework of the ruling institutions and their objectives (e.g., to discipline or gain profit), whereas tactics are the individual actions included in everyday activities such as walking, talking, and reading. Unlike strategies, tactics don't seek profits and aren't results of planning but depend on the situations and opportunities. They're the limited freedoms allowed by the framework of strategies. For this reason, de Certeau sees everyday practices as a form of political resistance: "The tactics of consumption" are "the ingenious ways in which the weak make use of the strong." For the de Certeau quotations here and in the text, see Michel de Certeau, *The Practice of Everyday Life* (University of California Press, 1988), xvii, 101.

7 Everyday Monuments

1 From Susan Sontag's speech upon being awarded the Friedenspreis des Deutschen Buchhandels (Peace Prize of the German Book Trade), Frankfurt Book Fair, October 12, 2003.

2 See Diane di Prima, "Revolutionary Letter #36," theanarchistlibrary.org/mirror/d/dd/diane-di-prima-revolutionary-letters.pdf.

3 Quoted in Janique Vigier, "Bernadette Mayer Remembers *Memory* (1971)," *Artforum*, May 25, 2020, artforum.com/columns/bernadette-mayer-remembers-memory-1971-247702.

4 Quoted in Fitzgerald, "Lives of the Poets: Bernadette Mayer," *Poetry Foundation*.

5 Bernadette Mayer, "Bring It Here," *Columbia: A Journal of Literature and Art*, no. 14 (1989), 104–08, JSTOR, jstor.org/stable/41807012?mag=everyday-life-revisted-with-bernadette-mayers-memory&seq=1.

6 Quoted in Andrew Epstein, "Bernadette Mayer's *Memory* as an Everyday-Life Project," WordPress.com, April 24, 2016, newyorkschoolpoets.wordpress.com/2016/04/24/bernadette-mayers-memory-as-an-everyday-life-project.

7 Bernadette Mayer, *Memory,* Eclipse Archive, originally published in 1976 by North Atlantic Books, eclipsearchive.org/projects/MEMORY/Memory.pdf.

8 See Rita Felski, *Doing Time: Feminist Theory and Postmodern Culture* (New York University Press, 2000), 19.
9 Lisa Robertson, *Boat* (Coach House Books, 2022), 120.
10 Susan Sontag, *Illness as Metaphor* (Farrar, Straus and Giroux, 1978), 50.
11 Bernadette Mayer, "Bernadette Mayer's List of Journal Ideas," University of Pennsylvania, writing.upenn.edu/library/Mayer-Bernadette_Experiments.html.
12 Mayer, *Midwinter Day*, 76.
13 Mayer, *Midwinter Day*, 67.
14 See Fanny Howe's observation of Bernadette Mayer's work at poetryfoundation.org/poets/bernadette-mayer.
15 Bronwen Tate, "The Day and the Life: Gender and the Quotidian in Long Poems by Bernadette Mayer and Lyn Hejinian," *Journal of Modern Literature* 40, no. 1 (2016): 42–64, doi.org/10.2979/jmodelite.40.1.03.
16 Amina Cain, *A Horse at Night: On Writing* (Dorothy, A Publishing Project, 2022), 96–97.
17 See Jean Rhys, *Smile Please: An Unfinished Autobiography* (Creative Arts, 1979), 5.
18 Mayer, "Bernadette Mayer's List of Journal Ideas."
19 Mayer, *Midwinter Day*, 52.

8 Books We Sleep With

1 Angela Carter, "The Company of Angela Carter," interview, *Marxism Today* (January 1985): 20–22.
2 Alejandro Zambra, *The Private Lives of Trees* (Open Letter, 2010), 33.
3 Leslie Adrienne Miller, "Alone in the Temple: A Personal Essay on Solitude and the Woman Poet," *Kansas Quarterly* 24/25, nos. 4/1 (1992–93): 200–214.
4 See "Mary Cassatt," Philadelphia Museum of Art," philamuseum.org/collection/curated/mary-cassatt.
5 There are many more paintings of Lydia reading, which we now might read as Mary Cassatt's tribute to her beloved sister, who

was already nursing the disease that killed her some years later at the age of forty-five. Cassatt drew her mother reading the daily paper as well, in a painting entitled *Reading "Le Figaro."*

6 For more on the Camille Sée Law, see Claire Goldberg Moses, *French Feminism in the 19th Century* (State University of New York Press, 1984), 32–33, 20.

7 William Godwin, *Memoirs of the Author of* A Vindication of the Rights of Woman (Garland, 1974), 64–65.

8 Mary Wollstonecraft, *A Vindication of the Rights of Woman*, rev. ed. (Penguin Books, 2004), 17.

9 In a letter to her sister Everina Wollstonecraft, November 7, 1787, Mary Wollstonecraft wrote: "Mr. Johnson … assures me that if I exert my talents in writing I may support myself in a comfortable way. I am then going to be the first of a new genus.… You know I am not born to tread in the beaten track — the peculiar bent of my nature pushes me on." "Mr. Johnson" was Joseph Johnson, her publisher. These quotes are from Don Paul Abbott's "'A New Genus': Mary Wollstonecraft and the Feminization of Elocution," *Rhetorica: A Journal of the History of Rhetoric*, 36, no. 3 (2018): 269–95.

10 Elena Ferrante, *My Brilliant Friend*, trans. Ann Goldstein (Text Publishing Company, 2015), 170.

11 Friedrich Nietzsche, *Untimely Meditations*, trans. R.J. Hollingdale (Cambridge University Press, 1983), 139.

12 Cain, *A Horse at Night*, 35.

13 For a study of these biases, see Hadiya Roderique's excellent article "Dating While Black," *The Walrus*, March 2017, thewalrus.ca/dating-while-black.

14 Laing, *The Lonely City*, 15.

15 Susan Sontag, *Reborn: Journals and Notebooks, 1947–1963* (Farrar, Straus and Giroux, 2008), 303.

16 Lucia Berlin, *A Manual for Cleaning Women* (Picador, 2015), 53.

17 See, for example, Sara Ahmed, *The Promise of Happiness* (Duke University Press, 2010), and Sianne Ngai, *Ugly Feelings* (Harvard University Press, 2007).

18 Ann Cvetkovich, *Depression: A Public Feeling* (Duke University Press, 2012).

19 Anne Carson, *Autobiography of Red* (McClelland & Stewart, 2016), 74.

20 Italo Calvino, *If on a Winter's Night a Traveller*, trans. William Weaver (Minerva, 1992), 156.

21 Lisa Robertson, *Nilling* (Book*hug, 2012), 26.

22 Lauren Berlant, *The Female Complaint: The Unfinished Business of Sentimentality in American Culture* (Duke University Press, 2008), 218.

9 This Is My World

1 Because of this lack of interference, some believe outsider art is more precious than the productions of professionals. For instance, the artist Jean Dubuffet believes the "exalted feverishness, lived so fully and so intensely by their authors" makes cultural art in its entirety appear "to be the game of a futile society, a fallacious parade" ("Place à l'incivisme [Make Way for Incivism]," *Art and Text*, no. 27 [December 1987–February 1988]: 36. In other words, there is something more authentic about art created in solitude and isolation than in the company of peers. But the line can't be so easily drawn.

2 See Rosa Lyster, "A Visit to South Africa's Strange, Astonishing Owl House," *The New Yorker*, February 1, 2018.

3 All details and excerpts from letters are from Susan Imrie Ross, *This Is My World: The Life of Helen Martins, Creator of the Owl House* (Oxford University Press, 1997).

4 Quoted in Anita Pollitzer, *A Woman on Paper: Georgia O'Keeffe* (Simon & Schuster, 1988), 229.

5 Quoted in Perry Miller Adao, *A Life in Art* (The Georgia O'Keeffe Museum, 2003), 14 min.

6 Some of these artists belonged to a loose collective known as the Precisionists, which had no interest in depicting humans or animals, just spaces, cities, and landscapes without people.

7 Quoted in Pollitzer, *A Woman on Paper*, 31, 26, 36.
8 Quoted in Pollitzer, *A Woman on Paper*, 48.
9 Stieglitz enjoyed his well-established routines; O'Keeffe felt that summers spent living with her in-laws cramped her work. O'Keeffe wanted a child; Stieglitz, who already had children, did not want more.
10 Letters from O'Keeffe to Stieglitz, Taos, NM, July 9, 1929. See Sarah Greenough, ed., *My Faraway One: Selected Letters of Georgia O'Keeffe and Alfred Stieglitz* (Yale University Press, 2011), and Nesha Ruther, "The Handwritten Love of Georgia O'Keeffe and Alfred Stieglitz," *Bond & Grace*, February 3, 2023, bondandgrace.com/lit-talk/the-handwritten-love-of-georgia-okeeffe-and-alfred-stieglitz.
11 Quoted in Katie Reilly, "Georgia O'Keeffe Reveals Inspiration Behind Some of Her Most Famous Paintings in Newly Uncovered Letters," *Time*, March 21, 2019, time.com/5555473/georgia-okeeffe-letters-library-of-congress/.
12 Patricia Norby, The Met's associate curator of Native American art, makes this critique. See "*Spotlight*: Revisiting O'Keeffe Country," November 3, 2022, metmuseum.org/perspectives/revisiting-okeeffe-country-faraway-nearby.

10 A Record of Girlhood

1 See Alice Munro, *The Progress of Love* (Penguin Canada, 2006).
2 Andrea Robin Skinner, "My Stepfather Sexually Abused Me When I Was a Child, My Mother, Alice Munro, Chose to Stay with Him," *Toronto Star*, July 7, 2024, updated July 4, 2025, thestar.com/opinion/contributors/my-stepfather-sexually-abused-me-when-i-was-a-child-my-mother-alice-munro-chose/article_8415ba7c-3ae0-11ef-83f5-2369a808ea37.html.
3 Alice Munro, "Miles City, Montana," in *The Progress of Love*, 113.
4 Alice Munro, *Runaway* (Vintage, 2005), 53.
5 Munro, *Runaway*, 135.
6 Munro, *Runaway*, 158.

7 Louise Glück, "Nostos," in *Meadowlands* (Carcanet, 1998), 43.
8 Virginia Woolf, *The Waves* (Harcourt, 1959), 64.

11 The Artist's City

1 Clara Pasieka, "Decades-Old Toronto Non-Profit Leasing Space to Artists Goes into Receivership," *Toronto Star*, August 29, 2023, cbc.ca/news/canada/toronto/artscape-receivership-1.6950825.
2 Zach Dubinsky, "Loblaws in $400M Tax Fight with CRA over Claims It Set Up Bogus Offshore Bank," *CBC News*, January 17, 2018, cbc.ca/news/business/loblaws-cra-glenhuron-bank-barbados-tax-1.4490564.
3 See Small Cap Steve, "How Loblaws' Galen Weston Doubled His Wealth At Your Expense," The Deep Dive, February 4, 2023, thedeepdive.ca/how-loblaws-galen-weston-doubled-his-wealth-at-your-expense.
4 Alice Constance Austin, "Building a Socialist City," *The Western Comrade* 4, no. 6 (October 1916): 17.
5 Jane Jacobs, *The Death and Life of Great American Cities* (Random House, 1961), 238.

Postscript

1 Woolf, "Professions for Women," 1942.
2 Woolf, "Professions for Women," 1942.

Bibliography

Albright, Alice P. "Gertrude Stein at Radcliffe: Most Brilliant Women Student." *The Harvard Crimson*, February 18, 1959.

Battersby, Christine. *Gender and Genius: Towards a Feminist Aesthetics*. Indiana University Press, 1989.

Beauvoir, Simone de. *The Second Sex*. Edited and Translated by H.M. Parshley. Vintage Books, 1989.

Berger, John. *Ways of Seeing*. British Broadcasting Corporation and Penguin Books, 1972.

Berlin, Lucia. *A Manual for Cleaning Women*. Picador, 2015.

Britt, Ryan. "The Toni Morrison Quote Every Parent Needs to Read." *Fatherly*, August 6, 2019. fatherly.com/love-money/the-toni-morrison-quote-every-parent-needs-to-read.

Cain, Amina. *A Horse at Night: On Writing*. Dorothy, A Publishing Project, 2022.

Calvino, Italo. *If on a Winter's Night a Traveller*. Translated by William Weaver. Minerva, 1992.

Carrington, Leonora. *The Complete Stories of Leonora Carrington*. Dorothy Project, 2017.

———. *Down Below*. *The New York Review of Books*, 2017.

Carson, Anne. *Autobiography of Red*. McClelland & Stewart, 2016.

Carter, Angela. *Nights at the Circus*. Penguin, 1986.

———. "Notes from the Front Line." In *On Gender and Writing*. Edited by Micheline Wandor. Pandora, 1983.

Certeau, Michel de. *The Practice of Everyday Life*. University of California Press, 1988.

Chopin, Kate. *The Awakening*. Herbert S. Stone & Company, 1899.

Currey, Mason. *Daily Rituals: How Artists Work*. Alfred A. Knopf, 2013.

Cusk, Rachel. "Can a Woman Who Is an Artist Ever Just Be an Artist?" *New York Times Magazine*, November 7, 2019. nytimes.com/2019/11/07/magazine/women-art-celia-paul-cecily-brown.html.

Cvetkovich, Ann. *Depression: A Public Feeling*. Duke University Press, 2012.

Dickinson, Emily. *The Poems of Emily Dickinson: Reading Edition*. Edited by Ralph W. Franklin. Harvard University Press, 1999.

Elkin, Lauren. *Art Monsters: Unruly Bodies in Feminist Art*. Farrar, Straus and Giroux, 2023.

Felski, Rita. *Doing Time: Feminist Theory and Postmodern Culture*. New York University Press, 2000.

Ferrante, Elena. *My Brilliant Friend*. Translated by Ann Goldstein. Text Publishing Company, 2015.

Fitzgerald, Adam. "Lives of the Poets: Bernadette Mayer." *Poetry Foundation*, April 4, 2011. poetryfoundation.org/articles/69658/lives-of-the-poets-bernadette-mayer.

Fletcher, Angus. *Allegory: The Theory of a Symbolic Mode*. Cornell University Press, 1964.

Garber, Megan. "David Foster Wallace and the Dangerous Romance of Male Genius." *The Atlantic*, May 8, 2018. theatlantic.com/entertainment/archive/2018/05/the-world-still-spins-around-male-genius/559925.

Giuffrida, Angela. "Italy: Proposal for Statue of First Woman to Get PhD Sparks Debate." *The Guardian*, January 3, 2022. theguardian.com/world/2022/jan/03/italy-proposal-statue-elena-cornaro-piscopia-first-woman-phd-debate.

Glück, Louise. "Nostos." In *Meadowlands*. Carcanet, 1998.
———. *A Village Life*. Carcanet, 2010.
Godwin, William. *Memoirs of the Author of A Vindication of the Rights of Woman*. Garland, 1974.
Hartman, Saidiya. "An Unnamed Girl: A Speculative History." *The New Yorker*, February 9, 2019.
hooks, bell. "The Oppositional Gaze: Black Female Spectator." In *Feminist Film Theory: A Reader*. Edited by Sue Thornham. New York University Press, 1999.
———. *Remembered Rapture: The Writer at Work*. Henry Holt, 1999.
Jacobs, Jane. *The Death and Life of Great American Cities*. Random House, 1961.
Jones, Radhika. "Toni Morrison as Editor Brought to Life Books by Muhammad Ali, Angela Davis, and Gayl Jones." *Vanity Fair*, August 8, 2019.
Ketchikan Visitors Bureau. "Ketchikan Story Project," 2016. ketchikanstories.com/ketchicon/chief-johnsons-totem-pole/totem-pole?slide=7.
Kincaid, Jamaica. *Lucy*. Farrar, Straus and Giroux, 1990.
Kristeva, Julia. "Is There a Feminine Genius?" *Critical Inquiry* 30, no. 3 (Spring 2004): 493.
Laing, Olivia. *The Lonely City: Adventures in the Art of Being Alone*. Picador, 2016.
Lefebvre, Henri. *Everyday Life in the Modern World*. Transaction Books, 1971.
Lispector, Clarice. *The Hour of the Star*. New Directions, 2020.
Mayer, Bernadette. *Midwinter Day*. New Directions, 1999.
Morrison, Toni. *Sula*. Vintage, 2004.
Moses, Claire Goldberg. *French Feminism in the 19th Century*. State University of New York Press, 1984.
Mulvey, Laura. "Visual Pleasure and Narrative Cinema." *Screen* 16, no. 3 (Autumn 1975): 6–18.
Munro, Alice. *Dance of the Happy Shades*. McGraw-Hill Ryerson, 1968.

———. *Lives of Girls and Women*. McGraw-Hill Ryerson, 1971.
———. *Munro's Best: Selected Stories*. McClelland & Stewart, 2006.
———. *The Progress of Love*. Penguin Canada, 2006.
———. *Runaway*. Vintage, 2005.
Nelson, Maggie. *The Argonauts*. Graywolf Press, 2015.
Nietzsche, Friedrich. *Untimely Meditations*. Translated by R.J. Hollingdale. Cambridge University Press, 1983.
Norby, Patricia Marroquin, and Matthew Martinez. "Revisiting 'O'Keeffe Country.'" Metropolitan Museum of Art, November 3, 2022. metmuseum.org/perspectives/revisiting-okeeffe-country-faraway-nearby.
Offill, Jenny. *Dept. of Speculation*. Alfred A. Knopf, 2014.
Okeowo, Alexis. "How Saidiya Hartman Retells the History of Black Life." *The New Yorker*, October 19, 2020.
Olsen, Tillie. *Silences*. Delacorte Press/Seymour Lawrence, 1978.
Pattee, Fred Lewis. *A History of American Literature Since 1870*. The Century Company, 1915.
Philadelphia Museum of Art. "Mary Cassatt." philamuseum.org/collection/curated/mary-cassatt.
Plath, Sylvia. *The Bell Jar*. Faber and Faber, 1966.
Pollitzer, Anita. *A Woman on Paper: Georgia O'Keeffe*. Simon & Schuster, 1988.
Rhys, Jean. *Good Morning, Midnight*. Shoreline Books, 1986.
———. *Smile Please: An Unfinished Autobiography*. Creative Arts, 1979.
———. *Voyage in the Dark*. Penguin Books, 1975.
———. *Wide Sargasso Sea*. Penguin Books, 2000.
Robertson, Lisa. *Boat*. Coach House Books, 2022.
———. *Nilling*. Book*hug, 2012.
Schappell, Elissa, and Claudia Brodsky Lacour. "Toni Morrison, the Art of Fiction, No. 134." *The Paris Review* 128 (Fall 1993). theparisreview.org/interviews/1888/the-art-of-fiction-no-134-toni-morrison.
Scott, Gail. *Spaces Like Stairs: Essays*. Women's Press, 1989.

Shraya, Vivek. *I'm Afraid of Men*. Penguin Canada, 2018.

Silko, Leslie Marmon. *Ceremony*. Penguin Books, 1977.

Skinner, Andrea Robin. "My Stepfather Sexually Abused Me When I Was a Child, My Mother, Alice Munro, Chose to Stay with Him." *Toronto Star*, July 7, 2025, updated. thestar.com/opinion/contributors/my-stepfather-sexually-abused-me-when-i-was-a-child-my-mother-alice-munro-chose/article_8415ba7c-3ae0-11ef-83f5-2369a808ea37.html.

Smith College Museum of Art. "Performed Invisibility: Ana Mendieta's 'Siluetas.'" Smith College Museum of Art, January 10, 2013. scma.smith.edu/blog/performed-invisibility-ana-mendietas-siluetas.

Sontag, Susan. *Illness as Metaphor*. Farrar, Straus and Giroux, 1978.

———. *Reborn: Journals and Notebooks, 1947–1963*. Farrar, Straus and Giroux, 2008.

Stein, Gertrude. *The Autobiography of Alice B. Toklas*. Penguin, 2020.

Unger, Miles J. *Picasso and the Painting That Shocked the World*. Simon & Schuster, 2018.

Walker, Alice. *In Search of Our Mothers' Gardens: Womanist Prose*. Harcourt, 2004.

Warner, Marina. *Monuments & Maidens: The Allegory of the Female Form*. Atheneum, 1985.

Wollstonecraft, Mary. *The Female Reader*. Scholars' Facsimiles & Reprints, 1980.

———. *A Vindication of the Rights of Woman*. Rev. ed. Penguin Books, 2004.

Woolf, Virginia. "Professions for Women." In *The Norton Anthology of Literature by Women: The Tradition in English*. 3rd ed., vol. 2. W.W. Norton, 2007.

———. *A Room of One's Own*. Penguin Books, 2004.

———. *The Waves*. Harcourt, 1959.

Zambra, Alejandro. *The Private Lives of Trees*. Open Letter, 2010.

Image Credits

8 Public domain

16 Public domain

83 Molly LaMorte

131 (*top to bottom; left to right*) Kasia Van Schaik, Eliza Robertson, Emmanuelle Sainté, Paige Cooper, Sunita Nigam, T. Liem, Sarah Bernstein, Annie Goh, and Dzitka Edwards

Index

Names followed by an asterisk are fictional characters.

About the Author

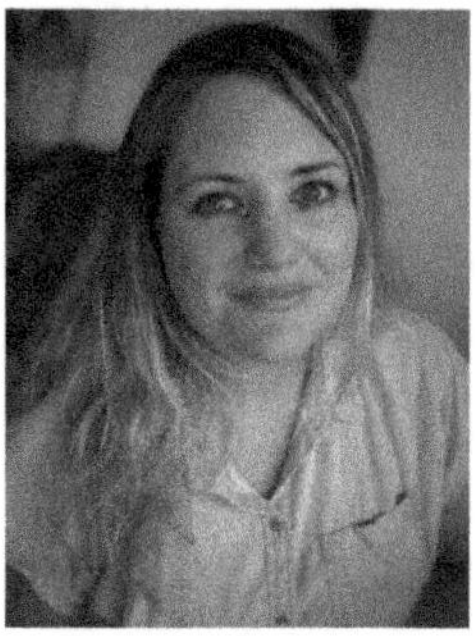

KASIA VAN SCHAIK WAS BORN IN South Africa and immigrated to Canada as a child. She is the author of the linked story collection *We Have Never Lived on Earth*, which was longlisted for the Giller Prize and shortlisted for the Concordia University First Book Prize and the ReLit Award for Short Fiction. Her other publications include the poetry chapbook *Sea Burial Laws According to Country* and the co-edited essay collection *Shelter in Text: Essays on Dwelling and Refuge*. Her writing has appeared in *Electric Literature*, the *Los Angeles Review of Books*, the *Best Canadian Poetry*, and the CBC. Kasia holds an M.A. in English in the field of creative writing from the University of Toronto and a Ph.D. in English literature from McGill University. She is assistant professor of English and co-director of creative writing at the University of New Brunswick. She lives in Fredericton, Wolastoqiyik territory.